EARTH'S ASCENSION
NIBIRU AND THE SPIRIT REALM

By Carl Franklin

EARTH'S ASCENSION - NIBIRU AND THE SPIRIT REALM
By Carl Franklin
ortcarl@aol.com
© 2018

ISBN-13: 978-0-9886851-9-2

The Mystic's Heart Publishing
12841 Hillcrest NE
Lowell MI 49331
USA

Themysticsheart.com

Bonnie, Thank You
for you to increase the
light on earth!

Carl

TABLE OF CONTENTS

DEDICATION

This book is dedicated to my beautiful, wise, angelic wife, Ortrun. She has been my companion, teacher, and helpmate for over 40 years. Without her, I would not be the person I am, and it is doubtful this book, or most of the spiritual activities we've participated in would have been accomplished. She has taught me to love. She is my soul mate and the love of my life!

ACKNOWLEDGEMENTS

Denise Iwaniw Francisco	*Publisher / Editor*
Todd Francisco	*Editor*
Alan Tutt	*Layout*
Jo E. Retzler	*Editor*
David Fix	*Graphic Arts (cover)*

I would like to give special thanks to our friend Denise Iwaniw Francisco. Her guidance and knowledge provided me with the motivation for writing and publishing this book.

ABOUT THE AUTHOR

I was a Lutheran minister in my mid-30s and had recently received a master's degree in Psychology. One of my professors had lightly touched on the subconscious mind. He said it was the largest portion of our mind. I felt there had to be a reason for having this subconscious mind and I vowed to learn to use it.

A short time later a Jesuit monk came into my life and became my mentor. He had left his religious order and was earning his livelihood as a hypnotist in surgical theaters working with patients who could not take anesthetics. He was a master of the subconscious mind. I learned about meditation from him and began to meditate daily and soon began to receive my sermons in the meditative state. Within two years I had outgrown the Lutheran beliefs and would have to leave if I was to continue on this new spiritual path. And with that came the end of my first marriage.

My spiritual life grew at a rapid rate. Two years later I married Ortrun, and together we have been traveling the spiritual metaphysical path. We both became Coptic ministers and quickly joined the spiritual metaphysical community in Grand Rapids, Michigan. For the last forty-plus years we have been teaching, leading seminars, doing private readings and giving talks. Ortrun and I work closely with Denise Iwaniw Francisco, a born seer, following the Native American spiritual path as a sacred pipe carrier. Together we lead a class called "The Mystery School". During these years my spiritual knowledge has come from many sources: my personal channelings, the channelings of others that I read, doing over 3,000 life script readings for people on the spiritual path, and becoming Santa Claus during the December holidays, which allowed me to be with over 25,000 children over the last 14 years.

For the past 35 years, I have worked daily with those we consider to be dead who are asking for help to be moved from the astral plane on to the heavenly realm. With this work I have learned about not only about what death is and what follows, but also what we are as humans.

Another part of my education has come from raising five children who have now blessed us with eleven grandchildren. Some of these children carry Crystal and Indigo energies. My family and spiritual metaphysics has been the focal point of my life for over 45 years and I feel so blessed and guided. It is my privilege to be able to share what I have learned with you for your thoughtful consideration.

As you read this you may sense the presence of unseen beings. They will likely be beings who have been with you most of your life. You usually are not aware of them until you are ready. In the meditative state you can communicate with them. I call them my "spirit family" and most of the channeled messages I get come from them. Life has been a fascinating and educational adventure. I hope sharing what I have learned can help you on your life journey.

INTRODUCTION

Much of the information in this book may be new to many of the readers. The reason is it is not coming from usual sources. For the last 45 years I have meditated at least once a day and, in that state, I am working out of both my conscious and subconscious minds together. It is called the alpha state, where the brain is operating at between 8 and 13 brain waves per second, whereas in our normal awake state our brain is functioning at around 22 brain waves per second. In the conscious state our focus is on all the information coming to us through our five senses. Our conscious mind, being far smaller than our subconscious mind, is kept busy processing all of this information plus dealing with our thoughts and emotions. The subconscious mind deals with what is within us that we are not aware of, and what is beyond the range of our five senses and the conscious mind. It is like developing a sixth sense.

Much of the information in this book has come in meditation or from the many-channeled messages I have read. The rest comes primarily from personal experiences and books and articles I have read. All information, including channeled, come from levels of consciousness. I will be sharing with you primarily those that have come from the higher levels and resonated with me to be true. Also, some of the personal experiences that I will be sharing with you have occurred in the meditative state and would not have been possible had I been in the awakened state.

In reading this book your logical conscious mind is going to be challenged because it will need to go beyond what it has experienced or may even logically thinks is possible. To get the most out of what you are going to be reading I strongly suggest that you keep your mind open and listen with your mind and heart working together. I also suggest that you read it as a book of possibilities, not facts, labeling what you have read from highly probable to highly improbable.

I have had a lifelong interest in science and documented as much as I can with physics, quantum physics, astrophysics, astronomy and research on death and dying. I have also drawn from *The Urantia Book* and the Bible and the writings of the international spiritual teacher Owen K Waters. I hope that what I have written has not been overly influenced by living in a Christian culture, please be aware of that possibility. I feel my forte is to connect dots coming from a wide range of sources, not only those that are in the physical realm but also those that are in the spirit realm. I feel, and have been told by others, that I walk in both of these worlds. In this book I am attempting to connect them and make it so you can sense the new world that is emerging, and that our descendants and we will occupy.

In this new world, people will be functioning at a higher level of consciousness, and the planet itself would be at operating a higher frequency, the frequency of love instead of fear. This transition has already begun! In the pages ahead, you will read not only about what has happened but also about what is slated to happen. You are not only going to experience these changes; each of us has a role to play in bringing these changes about. This information can help you understand the why behind what is happening and be better prepared to make the transition.

A word of warning: thoughts are energy, and if you fear, that fear energy is going to help create what it is you are afraid of. It is important that in the days, months and years ahead, you take responsibility for the thoughts you are holding in your mind, and focus only on what you want for yourself, your family, your community, and your world. These positive thoughts will help bring that into physical reality. Thank you for your help in doing this, and please enjoy the book.

Chapter 1

THE CREATION

How did the universe in which we live come into existence? What is it made of? Who designed it? I would like to share a perspective with you that answers these questions. Though I call it a perspective it resonates with me as being truth. Let's see how it resonates with you.

Most of my information about the Creator, the creation of our universe and the information about the three creations comes from *The Urantia Book*. The information in its 2,197 pages comes from the highest sources I have encountered. For me it feels true and if you read it you will find it is light years ahead of our current scientific knowledge.

Before our universal creator arrived, energy workers had been at work for a very long time gathering, creating, massaging and balancing the frequencies of many types of energy. These are the energies from which the universe would be created. When the proper amount, blend, and consistency of energy had been attained a Creator Son came from paradise to design and build our universe. The Creator Sons are created out of the consciousness and energy of Father God and Son God. Each Creator Son is unique because the blend of Father and Son consciousness and energy is unique in each one. Our

Creator son whose name is Christ Michael has more of the Son's energy than the Father's.

It is important to understand that since Christ Michael came from paradise. He had only known perfection. In creating his universe, it would be impossible to create anything better than what he came from. The fact that he created the universe as we know it to be indicates that he was curious and wanted to experience everything, even what was less than perfection. In this way he could expand his experience and knowledge. Owen Waters teaches that curiosity is a strong trait of The Creator of our universe and our experience tells us that this trait was passed on to us.

There are five basic factors that Christ Michael employed in designing and creating the universe. These five factors determine the nature and character of our universe and affect all life and experiences in the universe. They are:

1. Consciousness

2. Free will

3. Curiosity

4. Duality

5. Law of Cause and Effect

Note that the first four factors are in us and the last one is an inescapable trait of the universal environment in which everything exists. All five of these factors come out of *love* and allow *love* to be expressed through them. Love is the guiding force in all five factors that shape our ever-evolving universe. Now let's look at each one of these five factors so we can better understand not only the role they play in the operation of the universe, but also the role they play in our personal life remembering the underlying foundation of love.

Consciousness

Consciousness is present in everything that makes up the universe. Recent findings in quantum physics have helped to bring this to the surface. Much of the current discussion in quantum physics around consciousness got its start with the double-slit experiment. Experimenters found that depending upon the experiment run and the expected outcome, the light could display characteristics of a particle or a wave. Prior to this the thought was this should not be possible. This was run in different labs around the world with the same result. Many point to this as the start of the field of quantum physics and mechanics. To date no one has been able to give an exact reason for this and other strange characteristics seen at the smallest scale of existence, but many quantum physicists are pointing to consciousness being the piece that brings it all together.

Another example of strange behavior is Entanglement. Physicists have observed that particles can become entangled and act as one, even across vast distances. What happens to one immediately (no time gap) happens to the other. This puzzled Einstein. He called it "spooky action at a distance". Science only knows this happens; they don't know why. To me this is another sign that the entire universe is connected because it all exists in a field of consciousness! It is all *One*!

Because everything physical is made out of energy, according to the physicists, and light is energy, to me it is certain that everything has consciousness. The implications of this are mind stretching.

If we have consciousness, which we certainly do, and everything around us, including the cells in our physical body has consciousness, the potential exists that we can communicate with virtually everything. The implications for all types of science and for us in our everyday life are limitless. If we, and everything, has consciousness and free will, why aren't we communicating with everything? The answer is *we can* if we desire and know how to!

This explains how historical figures whom we regarded as holy or extraordinary were able to manifest material objects, perform healing, resurrect the dead, move their physical bodies from a place to place and other acts that were beyond the understanding, not only of the people of their day, but beyond our understanding today. This gives reason to believe that we may have the potential, each of us, of becoming a miracle worker.

Free Will

Free will is the companion of the consciousness. All consciousness has free will. Our consciousness gives us awareness of our self and what is around. Free will gives us the choice of how we choose to interact with the environment that we are in. Because consciousness is present in everything in the universe it too has the ability to choose how it responds to its surroundings. Free will opens the door to infinite possibilities in a multidimensional universe that we are barely beginning to understand.

Free will is limited by the physical nature of the vehicle that the consciousness is expressing through. Since our human physical bodies have larger brains, we have a greater potential for more free will than the over one million other living species on Earth. But even we are limited by our physical body and its five senses, which can only sense what is made of electromagnetic energy in which we experience in gaseous, liquid or solid form.

Thankfully our physical body houses three other aspects of us, mental, emotional and spiritual, to deal with the many other components in our life. We will go much deeper in understanding these 'other' aspects in the chapter on "What It Means to Be a Human Being".

Curiosity

Curiosity is what motivates us to use our free will. Curiosity is stronger in the human race than any other life form on the planet. We are certainly the most inventive socially, scientifically, technologically, economically, religiously, etc. Our curiosity has allowed us to evolve way beyond any other species. Without curiosity we could still be hunter/gatherers living in caves. Curiosity is what motivates us to always find a better way, a more efficient way, an easier way. It is what is behind our always asking why, how, what, where and even when. It is a trait, which if we lacked, would make us little more than just a physical human body.

These three traits, consciousness, free will, and curiosity, play major roles in making us what and who we are. The next two factors we discuss will deal with what is outside of us that shapes the universal environment in which we exist.

Duality

Duality allows for virtually all possibilities to be experienced. This allows us and the Creator to experience that what is less than perfection in an infinite variety of situations. It allows the universe to be a dynamic school in which nothing is static and new possibilities are constantly being explored and knowledge is growing at an unimaginable rate. It is duality that allows for all opposites to coexist, good and evil, life-and-death, creation and destruction, light and dark, big and small, hot and cold, etc. In other words, most anything is possible.

Can you imagine living in a universe where duality is not present? Because I've never experienced it and really, I can't even begin to imagine what it would be like. I only know it would not be as exciting as a universe with duality.

Duality also poses a high level of risk when linked with consciousness, free will, and curiosity. This opens the possibility for beings of higher intelligence to misuse the energy out of which the universe is created. It could be used to destroy life forms, planets, even galaxies. They could get so hung up on power that there would be no end to the destruction they could cause. To try to guide how free will is used without limiting freedom is the intent of the fifth factor, the law of cause and effect.

Law of Cause and Effect

The law of cause and effect, as stated by Sir Isaac Newton, "for every action there is an equal and opposite reaction." And, as stated by Jesus, "As you sow, so shall you reap." There is no way this law of cause and effect can be avoided. Every thought, emotion, word, and action carries with it a consequence. No intelligent and mentally healthy person would choose to harm them self. They would do that which brings the results they desire. This is the effect of the law of cause and effect.

But there are people, whose focus is only on their self, who desire and work toward goals that are beneficial to them but harmful to other people or to nature. This is a weakness in the law that throughout our history has caused much pain, death, and destruction to people and planets.

People whose value system and consciousness are "service to self" almost always cause this destructive behavior. Their focus is on themselves. If they benefit from it, in their mind it is good. Because they do not think beyond themselves about the affects it will have on others, they are of a limited consciousness. They lack love, the key component unifying the universe.

To have a better world the solution becomes obvious: we need to help people grow to a higher level of consciousness, to a consciousness of service to others, helping them to consider the long-term effect that their actions will have on others and the planet that sustains our physical bodies - in other words, a consciousness of love. It is a problem that requires training, education, and spiritual growth.

Of these five basic elements used to create the universe I find consciousness the most intriguing. The only place consciousness could have come from is The Creator himself. In my mind, I see the energy out of which the universe was about to be made and The Creator with the plan in his mind sending his thoughts and loving consciousness into the energy. The energy is now *one* with the Creator's love, consciousness, free will, curiosity, duality and the law of cause and effect. As The Creator places his consciousness in this field of energy, it becomes what the scientists call "The Big Bang", and the universe comes into being. In my mind the universe is the body of the Creator in which He experiences all that happens.

This makes the universe the ever-expanding consciousness of The Creator, a universe in which an infinite variety of life forms can have untold experiences in any of the eleven dimensions. In each and every experience of each and every being The Creator's consciousness is present and The Creator's knowledge and understanding of duality is increasing. The Creator is getting exactly what he wanted.

To broaden his experience The Creator created a universe with 11 different steps also called densities or dimensions. Astrophysicists have mathematically verified this. The five lower dimensions in which we live and experience with our five senses, are made primarily of electromagnetic energy. Dimensions six through eleven are made out of higher frequency energies that are beyond the range of our five senses. Astrophysicists refer to these higher dimensions as "dark matter or dark energy." These terms simply mean we know something is there, but we don't know what.

According to *The Urantia Book* the name of our universe is Nebadon and it is unimaginably huge! We have not yet found the outer edges of it and the scientists tell us it is still expanding, and the rate of expansion is increasing. In the five lower dimensions of the universe that we can see, the astronomers are telling us most galaxies have one to two billion stars, many with solar systems, and in recent articles in scientific journals scientists say there could be several billion up to one trillion galaxies in our universe. Our minds are not developed enough to be able to comprehend the enormity of this. And the fact that all of this is made of the same consciousness that we are is mind boggling! And this is only five of the 11 dimensions that make up the universe.

And all of this is just in one universe. Is this the only universe or are there more? Scientifically at this time this cannot be answered, but in *The Urantia Book*, which has been channeled from the highest sources I have ever read or encountered, there are answers. Drawing information from *The Urantia Book* we are now going to look at the totality of creation, which will give a much larger picture, a picture in which our universe makes up a very small part of the total creation. This is the only source for this type of information that I am aware of. At our level of consciousness and knowledge we can neither prove nor disprove what you are about to read, so I suggest you keep an open mind. I view it as possible.

CHAPTER 2

THE THREE CREATIONS

The First Creation Paradise

T he first creation is at the center of all three creations. It is a very large sphere called Paradise. This is the home of Father, Mother and Son God, the prime creators and overseers of all three creations. Paradise is the only thing in all of creation that is not moving. It is stationary and does not move. Everything else in creation is moving. Paradise acts as the axis around which everything else rotates. The Creators and their support staff utilize 10% of paradise. Ninety percent is reserved for the returning children of the Creators and presently less than 1% of that space is occupied. As you can well imagine everything in paradise and surroundings spheres is perfect.

Revolving around paradise are smaller spheres. On three of those spheres are children of the Creators that have or will be impacting our universe and us here on planet Earth. Each of these three spheres contains a different type of offspring of the Creators. They are:

1. The Creator Sons are created all of the energy and consciousness of Father God and Son God. The role they play is to create and oversee the universes in the third creation. Each creator son is unique with their own blend of father and son energies and consciousness, their own values and personalities.

2. On the second sphere are the Teacher Sons of God. They are created out of the energy and consciousness of Mother God and Son God. When a species is ready for them a Teacher Son of God will take on their physical form and be with them for an extended period of time helping them to achieve their next higher level in consciousness. They have not yet worked on Earth, but likely will sometime in the future.

3. The Magisterial Sons of god are created out of the energy and consciousness of Father God, Mother God, and Son God. They are the magistrates in the third creation settling disputes that might arise between universes, within universes, between galaxies, star systems, planets and species. Because of their versatility, they are also known as God's trouble-shooters working on any other assignment they are given. In certain situations, they also act as teachers. The inhabitants on the many other spheres rotating around paradise are not going to be interacting with us so I am not going to go into them.

The Second Creation

Solely, Father God created the second creation. He has worked on it for an extended period of time and has spent so much energy and thought that it is now perfect. No further improvements are possible. In that sense, it is a lot like life on paradise. Attributing human traits to Father God, I can't but wonder if like us, when he ends one project he begins another.

If it is perfect with no further improvements possible what is there left to do but to enjoy the fruits of his labor. I do believe that in creating the second creation father God honed his creative skills, which he then passed on to his creator sons to guide them in creating the third creation. In the back of my mind I can't help but wonder, if God honed his creative skills making the second creation, who created the first creation? I realize this is unanswerable, but I still wonder.

The second creation is shaped like a doughnut. Paradise, and its many spheres, exists in the hole of the doughnut. The doughnut rotates around paradise and *The Urantia Book* says it is exceedingly large, many times larger than our universe. The third creation then rotates around the second creation giving us a wheel inside a wheel rotating around the axis of paradise.

The Third Creation

Most of the information dealing with the creation of the third creation and the creation of our universe, known as *Nebadon*, comes from *The Urantia Book*. The third creation is composed of seven super universes. The first six super universes are complete with their full contingency of 100,000 universes each. We are in the seventh super universe, which has over 87,000 universes, but needs another 12,000-plus universes in order to be completed. When that occurs the third creation will be completed. This is not something to be concerned about at this time, as it will probably take seven to eight billion years to complete. When it is complete, not only will our seventh super universe be completed, but the entire third creation will have been completed. Some of the authors of *The Urantia Book* noted that there is a flurry of activity in a far distant area of space. A huge amount of energy is appearing and being worked on and this may be in preparation for the building of the fourth creation. But that is pure speculation as no announcement has yet been made.

Our universe, Nebadon, is one of the newer universes in our super universe. There are over 63,000 universes in our super-universe that are older than Nebadon. This means the beings living there have had more time to evolve in consciousness, spirituality, physicality, and technologically. If we viewed the oldest universe as a middle-aged adult, that would make Earth a late adolescent. Those on the even newer universes would still be in infancy to late childhood. To date we have not had the opportunity to compare ourselves to others but based on numerous channeled messages it appears that we soon will. The messages say we are getting close to being contacted and visited by some of our more advanced universal citizen.

The universe is a school for all of the creatures in the universe. They learn because the cause and effect experience reveals that what they think, feel and do brings about consequences.

Our learning is also assisted because we, Earth, the solar system, the galaxy, and even the universe are always moving into a different area of space and each area carries its own frequency of energy. Each new field of energy in Earth's 26,000-year cycle is represented by one of the twelve signs on the Zodiac and about 2,300 years long. Each 26,000 years (12 x 2,300) brings us to the next level in the spiral. Each age and each level allows us to have different experiences because the energy frequency is different. This is a part of The Creator's plan as it facilitates our growth and education by giving us the opportunity to use our free will and learn the results in ever-changing frequencies of energy.

It is interesting to note that several scientific journals have reported that a number of astrophysicists are saying that the universe appears to be following the same laws that govern holograms and that the entire universe may be a hologram. A hologram is a three-dimensional picture of pixels of light. The number of pixels per square inch determines the clarity and detail of the picture. One of the aspects of a hologram is that you can take any single pixel in the hologram and if you enlarge it sufficiently you will have the entire hologram.

In the same way the Creator placed his consciousness within every aspect of his creation. And because we are the most highly evolved species on the planet, could it be that more of the Creator's consciousness was placed in us. If the concept that the universe is a hologram is correct, our pixels of light (our soul) would be brighter than pixels of light in animals, plants, liquids, gases and minerals. There is some evidence that the ancients were aware of this.

Two examples are in the Bible. It is stated in Genesis that, "God created man in his own image and likeness. In his image and likeness, he created them." Jesus also asked us "Do you not know that you are God?"

When Christ Michael was created out of the energy and consciousness of Father God and Son God, he carried more of the Son's energy than the Father's energy. This was perhaps a factor when he came to create his own universe. The only thing Christ Michael had experienced prior to coming here was perfection. By definition, it is impossible to create anything better than perfection. What he had never experienced was imperfection. This fact along with his having more of the Son's energy may have made him a little more daring in creating his own universe. This universe allows him the opportunity to experience and experiment with duality.

Duality is the very nature of our universe. To me this is the understanding I have of the story of Adam and Eve who ate from the tree of knowledge, of good and evil, in other words, the tree of duality. Adam and Eve could not escape the consequence of their choice to eat of the fruit of good and evil. Their eyes were opened, and they found they were in a world of duality. The story, for me, is attempts to explain why both good and evil exist in the world.

In trying to understand why our universe is as it is, please keep in mind that when Christ Michael came He was, in essence, placed in a sand box of energy where he could create anything that he desired. The energy had the potential to become whatever was put into it, just as a stem cell in our physical body can become any type of cell. Christ Michael chose to fill the open vessels of energy, that would become His and our universe with *love,* expressing as consciousness, curiosity, duality and free will. The law of cause and effect was added to guide how free will is used and making it a teaching tool without controlling free will.

The law of cause and effect creates a safety valve for how free will is used in a world of duality. Most intelligent healthy beings are not going to do those things that are harmful to themselves, and as they grow in consciousness they will not do that which is harmful to others or to the environment that nourishes and supports them. However, to me it is apparent there is the potential danger that creatures who only look out for themselves with disregard for others, when they develop technology they can pose a danger to many, even an entire planet.

We now have the technology to destroy all life on Earth and the implications of this are mind-boggling. I think that for many who are reading this book the reason you and I are on Earth at this crucial time is to see that this does not happen! We will go deeper into this in a later chapter.

CHAPTER 3

THE ASCENSION OF EARTH AND HUMANITY

Ascension Background

The universe has a problem that has been going on for a very long time. The basis of the problem is free will. In the mind of The Creator free will is a key component in the creation of the universe, it fosters curiosity, which leads to creativity. In his writings, Owen Waters says that it was The Creator's curiosity that played a key role in the Creator creating the universe as it is. He had never experienced imperfection and it was his curiosity about imperfection that led him to create a universe of duality, in which everything has consciousness and free will.

In this universe all things would be able to use its free will to express itself any way it chose, limited only by its nature. It would of course experience the results of that action, good or bad, because of the law of cause and effect. Thus, the consequences of thoughts, emotions, words and actions would always be felt. When you add in curiosity this creates a universe that will always be evolving and growing to become something greater then it is.

The alternative to free will is to have a universe governed by laws, rules, etc., with the Creator fully in charge. With free will it allows everyone/everything in the universe to influence not only its self but also its environment and, in the big picture, to ideally create the universe in a form that ideally supports the highest good for every aspect of the universe. On the other hand, it also opens the door to the possibility that things could go terribly wrong. Because free will is such a key component in our universe it is treated as though it is sacred. It cannot be removed or interfered with.

I believe the Creator anticipated that the unavoidable law of cause and effect upon which the universe functions would cause free will to be used in a way that was, in the long term, positive because one can never escape the effect of one's thoughts, feelings, words, and actions.

As mentioned earlier, in the world of physics, Sir Isaac Newton was one of the first to state "every action has an equal and opposite reaction." Everything in the universe is subject to this law. It can never be avoided. In the vast majority of cases behavior by any aspect of creation will not be repeated if it does not bring the desired results. However, there are situations where self-interest ignores the consequences for others. This tends to create larger problems for others to solve.

The misuse of free will has and continues to create a major problem in our universe. The universal Creator decided he wanted to find a solution to these situations. The problem is this; 75% of the planets in the universe when they are transitioning from the third dimension through the fourth and into the fifth dimension end up destroying all life on the planet and make the planet uninhabitable for virtually all life. This same, or similar, message has been reported in channelings from several highly respected chandlers over the last several decades.

The channeled messages report that the reasons this happens is:

1. The advanced society on the planet has developed their technology faster than their consciousness and spirituality. They have not grown enough in love and wisdom and misuse their technology.

2. The leaders, or those who control the technology, place their personal desires for power, wealth, etc., above their concern for their fellow beings or their planet.

The channeled messages go on to say that Christ Michael put out a call throughout the universe inviting planets that were inhabited with beings that were in the third-dimensional level of consciousness, and approaching the time of being able to move up into the fourth and then the fifth-dimensional level of consciousness, to volunteer to host an experiment. The purpose of the experiment was to come up with ways to assist third-dimensional planets through this transition safely.

Third-dimensional consciousness is based on fear, limitation and separation. These form the foundation of the values, beliefs, social institutions and behaviors of the society. The fifth-dimensional consciousness is based on love, at-one-ment and empowering each person so they can fully develop their potential. The fourth dimension is the transitional period.

Our beloved mother Earth is one of many planets throughout the universe that volunteered to host this experiment and was the one that the Creator chose. To assist Earth in hosting this experiment is one of the reasons our universal Creator, Christ Michael, came here in human form to lay the foundation for the ascension process that is going on now. We know him as Jesus the Christ. We will go into this in greater detail later in this book.

As stated in one word, that foundation that Jesus created is love. While here, Jesus said to, "Love one another even as I love you," that, "God is love," and to "Do unto others what you would have them do unto you." Love is the key component of building the foundation. When we humans raise our consciousness from the level of fear to love, love of self, love of others and love of our planet, a major step in the ascension process will have been completed.

The foundation that Jesus laid has two significant factors. The first is love and the many ways in which love can be expressed. He demonstrated that love could be a way of life. It begins with loving yourself and reaches out to others by being of service to them by encouraging and supporting them in developing their highest potentials; and also, by being forgiving and understanding, by sharing of our self and possessions, and by sensing the divine essence within our self and in all others.

The second thing he taught and showed us is who we are, and the potential that we have. As you know Jesus performed many, many miracles and healings, feeding the multitude, quieting the wind and waves, raising the dead, and his own resurrection. When asked who he was, Jesus stated, "I am the Son of Man." Like us, when he came he left his memory behind. He was as physical and human as we are and yet he was able to do all of these miraculous things. He also said of himself, "My Father and I are one." This is usually misunderstood as meaning he is the only son of God.

I would like to share a different meaning of his statement with you. I believe he meant that as a person he had become one with the divine essence within himself. In other words, he had become one with his soul, which is the divine essence found in each and every one of us. He said to us, "All of the signs and wonders you see me do, these and even greater you shall do." Jesus also asked, "Do you not know that you are God?" This is our potential.

In other words, you have a soul that is the divine consciousness within you and when you become one with it, allowing it to become one with you, you will have connected with your divine essence. Then you will be able to do all that Jesus did and even greater. When we reach this point in our life we will have personally ascended into the high end of the fifth dimension, which is the level of Christ consciousness. As we achieve this in our personal ascension, we will have ascended to the highest level of consciousness that can currently be reached on Earth. In doing this we will have assisted in raising the consciousness of humanity and our planet. This, to me, is the best and most powerful thing each of us can do to assist with the ascension.

The world that Jesus came into was deeply into the third-dimensional level of consciousness. This level is built on fear, limitation, and separation. As I write this in the spring of 2018, the collective consciousness of the human race during the holiday season in December 2017 moved out of the high end of the third dimension into the low end of the fourth dimension. However, all of our human institutions on the planet were created in, and remain in third-dimensional consciousness. This includes our governments, religions, economies, educational systems, healthcare systems, sciences, healthcare, and more.

The perception of many people I talk to and my personal observation along with numerous magazine articles and TV commentators are that many of these social institutions are on the verge of failing because they are not meeting people's expectations or needs.

There may be truth to this perception because, common sense, as well as numerous channelings, points out that the old must be upgraded or they will fail making room for their fifth-dimensional replacement. The fourth dimension is the time between the third and fifth. It is a time with rapid change and much chaos. The third-dimensional institutions will be failing, while the fifth dimensional ones will be emerging and growing. For a decade or so we will have both third-dimensional and fifth-dimensional institutions functioning. This should make life very interesting. It is important that during this time we do not focus on the chaos. This would keep you in fear, which is negative, does not solve anything, deepens the chaos, makes you unhappy and is harmful because it empowers what you are afraid of.

We need to focus on what we want to create to replace it. We are creators. Our ancestors created the third-dimensional institutions that are about to leave. We are to be the creators of the fifth-dimensional institutions and that can only be done with fifth-dimensional consciousness. Because all creation begins with thought empowered by positive emotion, especially the emotion *desire*, it is important that we stay positive and keep our focus on what we want.

Fifth-dimensional consciousness is based on:

1. Love, Love of self, love of others, love of all life, love of the planet and love of The Creator. Love is the foundation and unifying force of the universe. It always seeks the highest good for all.

2. At-one-ment. There is only one, and that is the consciousness and the love of The Creator. Everything in the universe is an aspect of the Creator. All is *one*.

3. Personal empowerment. This means empowering *all* people. It begins with self-empowerment and helping each person to reach their maximum potential. This includes guiding each person, so they have the opportunity to become one with their indwelling divine essence, their soul.

Close your eyes for a moment and envision a world where all are living out of a fifth-dimensional level of consciousness. Everyone is surrounded by other beings who love, support, and encourage them. The vast majority of people are helping to empower each other. There is no violence, there is much laughter, there are celebrations as goals are met and exceeded. There is no fear, no violence, hardly any criticism, very little physical, mental or emotional illness, no drugs, and most everybody is healthy. So much love and hugs abound. Respect for even the most unique and unusual beings is universal, and uniqueness is valued. People are living in two worlds, the physical world and the spirit world, communicating with plants and animals, with angels and Devas (nature spirits). It is as if Heaven and Earth have become one. This is what the mid to high end of the fifth dimension is like, one harmonious people living on a peaceful, loving, supportive planet that is loved and respected.

Ascension Plan

Yes, there is a plan to help us achieve Heaven and Earth. The plans are slowly being revealed to us, as we are ready to receive them by higher-dimensional space beings, the *Pleiadians*, the *Arcturians* and the *Sirians*. Please remember the larger plan is to find ways for plants to make the transition from third to the fifth dimension safely without destroying all life on the planet. To do this Earth needs to become like those planets that have destroyed all life on their surface. The causes have been identified on those planets, and we are to devise ways to solve, remove, modify or transform the causes in a peaceful non-destructive way. To do this we must have those same situations on Earth. Here are the steps in the plan.

Step One. Remove from the *surface* of Earth those things that could impede the implementation of the plan. This involved the removal of the Lemurian people from the surface of Earth over 25,000 years ago. They were simply too spiritually evolved and would have impeded step two of the plan. This was accomplished by having the Atlanteans threaten to invade Lemuria. The Lemurians were a peace-loving people, so peace-loving that they would not even defend themselves. They were highly evolved in their spiritual beliefs and practices and many of them had attained a high fifth-dimensional level and some even a sixth-dimensional level of consciousness. The plan called for the Lemurians to stay with Earth because they could be very helpful in building a fifth-dimensional culture and society on the coming fifth dimensional Earth.

In order to escape the threat from the Atlanteans, the six-dimensional Lemurians, who are nonphysical beings, having what we would call "spiritual bodies", created portals into Inner Earth, which the fifth and even high fourth-dimensional beings could utilize. Once the Lemurians were all in Inner Earth, they closed the portals, so they could not be followed. After they left their continent, it began sinking into the ocean and is now at the ocean bottom.

I have spoken with a few Inner Earth people who have come to Earth's surface to help with the ascension of Earth and her people and to keep Inner Earth leaders informed about events. We will not have full contact with our Inner Earth cousins until violence has ended.

The Atlanteans society and culture needed to be broken up because they were so technologically advanced that they could bring about the very demise of life on Earth before the timing was right. More time was needed to prepare Earth, that is, to set the stage, so Earth could play the role that it had volunteered to play.

Sometime after the Lemurian continent sank, Atlantis also began sinking. The Atlanteans that survived the sinking of their continent fled to many different regions of Earth. We know this because pyramids were built using Atlantean technology and are found throughout much of the world.

At this point, the stage had been cleared and Earth was ready for the next phase.

Step Two. Create the situations/conditions on Earth that leads to destroying life and making the planet uninhabitable. To do this, beings who are highly evolved technically, but not spiritually or in their consciousness, are invited to come to Earth to create the same conditions here that existed on the planets that destroyed life on their surface. This is going to be setting the stage for the final phase.

After the *plan* was complete and approved by Christ Michael a contract was signed with the beings referred to as the Illuminati, who were to duplicate the situations that existed on the planets where life was destroyed. It is important to note that the contract termination date was January 1, 2000. By that time the Illuminati's work was to have been completed and they were to leave. Most of the Illuminati chose to ignore that date and continue doing what it seems they had become addicted to, power, control, and wealth.

As of this writing, in the spring of 2018, channeled information says most all of the Illuminati have gone. However, their minions, that is, the humans that they trained, are still holding on to the governments, religions, economies, mass communication and other social structures developed by the Illuminati. The few remaining Illuminati's, and their minion's, control on these is becoming ever more tenuous. The trust of the people in these institutions is waning and the longing is increasing for something better, something that is more responsive and works more effectively. These longings are creating the instability in our economies and governments. These desires are the seeds that are soon to bloom.

Fear is the primary way that the Illuminati control us. They instigate situations that make us afraid. They benefit because fear is their primary source of energy, which is their basic food, and they obviously enjoyed the power to control and obtain wealth. They influence the kind of human behavior that led to cutting down the forests, which provides much of our oxygen, thus altering our atmosphere. They encouraged behaviors that polluted much of our water. They encourage the mining of coal and the drilling for oil and gas even though they knew this was injurious to our mother Earth. They help design instruments of war and killing, including nuclear bombs.

The Illuminati also played a major role in forming our religions and the beliefs that use fear to control us. Increasing numbers of people are leaving organized religion, thinking for themselves and connecting with the divine within. But please keep in mind that this was a part of the plan so that everything could culminate at the appropriate time.

War is a favorite weapon of the Illuminati. It creates a tremendous amount of fear allowing them to have a feast while at the same time generating power and wealth for themselves by devastating the environment and personal property. They manufacture war materials and equipment, allowing them to assert their power, creating a division and hatred among people, and keeping people at a survival level of consciousness. War is a way of keeping human consciousness at a low level, generating anger and guilt, as well as fear.

Another way the Illuminati create fear and exert their control is by influencing the weather. They have the ability to strengthen the power of hurricanes, to help create the conditions that favor the development of tornadoes, hurricanes, floods, and earthquakes. They fostered hydraulic fracturing (fracking) in the oil fields, which increases the frequency and severity of earthquakes.

They have, on Earth, all of the life-destroying situations that need to be present in a third-dimensional planet transitioning to the fourth dimension. The Illuminati have succeeded in fulfilling their part of the contract. You do not have to be super perceptive to see that we are at or very close to that point where in the right situation we could destroy all life on Earth. *Know this will not happen!* This is not something to be afraid of! Fear will only make the situation worse and is detrimental to you.

Rather it is the call to begin visualizing and emotionally feeling what it is you want in the world. In other words, the stage is fully set and we who are the actors in this play now need to assume our role, *the role of creator!*

Step Three. *Creating the new Earth (a new beginning).* This is beginning even while the chaos of clearing out the old third-dimensional thinking, acting and institutions is going on. Assisting us are four major components of the ascension that are happening in space. They are listed below and will be discussed in more detail in coming pages.

1. Earth is moving into the photon belt and needs to be in the belt more fully. *Science doesn't think photon belt exists or is possible*

2. Nibiru is a large planet with a 3,600-year elliptical orbit that is currently in our inner solar system and will go between Earth and Mars.

3. We need to be more fully in the Aquarian age. Currently we are in 56% Aquarian energy and 44% Piscean energy. Aquarian energy is higher frequency than Piscean energy. By the mid-2080s will be fully in the Aquarian age and with it the higher frequency Aquarian energies.

4. High frequency waves of energy are being sent to Earth from four-star systems - Pleiadians, Arcturians, Andromedans and Sirians. The vibrational frequency of the energy is increasing, and the waves are coming more often. These energies are assisting Earth to move thru the fourth dimension into the fifth dimension. Other waves are impacting Earths life forms, especially humans, improving physical bodies and raising levels of consciousness. As these four changes take place, they are each raising the frequency of Earth and creating a positive environment for higher human consciousness.

Let's look at these forthcoming changes in a little more detail.

Our solar system is entering what is called the photon belt. Earth goes through the photon belt every 26,000 years and it takes 2,000 years to completely go it. Photons are particles of light and the belt is made up of a high concentration of photons. This creates a field of high-frequency energy that Earth is now entering. *Science ≠ photon belt*

The further we go into it the denser the field becomes and the higher the frequency of the energy surrounding Earth becomes. When we combine this with entering into the higher energy of the Aquarian age, the waves of high frequency energy Earth is receiving, we getting a triple whammy! These three factors play an important role in assisting us to raise our personal and collective human consciousness and helping Earth to become a fifth-dimensional planet. It is these three energies that determine the timing of the ascension. That this is happening at the same time that we are going to have Nibiru passing by is no coincidence.

The timing as you can tell has been carefully planned. The curtain is rising, and the play is beginning. This information comes from multiple sources; channelings, science, family, our students, friends and my personal experience. We are all experiencing changes in our physical bodies (unexplained aches, fatigue, changes in sleep and energy patterns), our mental bodies (different thoughts, outlooks, responses, values; more open-minded and tolerant; less anger and judgment, etc.), our emotional bodies (happier, more peaceful, loving, self-confident, forgiving, peaceful, hopeful), in our spiritual life (through meditation; by seeing, hearing, feeling and or sensing the presence of nonphysical loving beings; by remembering events from past lives; by developing psychic abilities, etc.)

The changes have already begun on planet and the old creation is being either transformed or ending to make room for what seems like a new, vastly-improved Earth. We are in the beginning of a time of great confusion because two forces, two levels of consciousness, service to self and service to others, are overlapping - one weakening, and one growing stronger.

This is the hardest and most confusing time we will go through in the process of ascending from the third-dimensional level of consciousness into the fifth. This time in between time can be referred to as the fourth dimension, a time of exceedingly rapid change, a time of great confusion and uncertainty, and a time of both chaos and readiness for change.

Certainly, you are wondering about the timing of this great change. An exact date cannot be given for many of the events that will make up the whole ascension process, because there are too many variables, such as human free will.

Also, we are not talking about a single event. Ascension is an ongoing process throughout the universe. Because of *the plan,* ascension on Earth is greatly sped up. It will happen over generations instead of millenniums. For instance, if we lose land due to the rising waters resulting from climate change, we will need to build structures that will take those waters and make them work for us, perhaps as new sources of energy. The time of "chaos" becomes the time we change the fastest for the betterment of Earth and all beings here, because love will be more prevalent and stronger than fear.

Just a reminder that what you have and will be reading is one person's perspective. What resonates true for me may resonate differently with you. I suggest you read this as a book of possibilities rather than facts. The information is coming from science, the Bible, *The Urantia Book*, many channelings and personal experiences. All information coming from these sources is subject to interpretation. I encourage you to be discerning, accepting what sounds and feels true, modify what does not, so it fits your own beliefs and reject what does not resonate with you.

It's important to note that the ascension is not a single event, but a series of events that began roughly 25,000 years ago with the sinking of the Lemurian and then the Atlantean continents. The process began speeding up in the mid-1930s and has been coming at an ever-faster rate ever since.

Regarding the ascension, the mid-1930s were noteworthy because, first, *The Urantia Book* was given to us by extremely highly evolved beings. An anonymous dentist in Chicago went into a trance state under the observation of a physician and a psychiatrist, and channeled it all. The doctors found the information so fascinating they hired a stenographer who recorded all of the sessions that were held three evenings a week for three years.

The information was so far beyond science and the consciousness level at that time that they were reluctant to publish it. The Urantia Society finally published it in 1955. Check within yourself to see if you are ready to read it, and if you are, please read it in reverse order. The book has four parts. Read part four first and then parts three, two, and one. Parts one, two and three do not take place on Earth and the language does not exist to adequately communicate what they are trying to say. Reading it backwards you slowly back into their language.

Second, in the mid-1930s the number of people coming into the world with advanced DNA, that is more than 20 active codons in their DNA, began to increase. Our DNA looks like a twisted stepladder and the rungs are the codons. Historically it is estimated only 1% of the human population had more than 20 active codons in their DNA. Those that did were the leaders, the innovators, often of the political, religious and military rulers, many of whom were largely controlled by the Illuminati. This is evident by their horrific actions recorded in the history books. These same leaders are the ones who, under the Illuminati's guidance, created current social institutions that are to be transformed or replaced.

Since the mid-1930s the change in our DNA has been dramatic! Going from approximately 2% to over 60% in 2018! Geneticists have verified the increase but not the percent of increase. I began being a Santa in 2002 and have had over 25,000 children sit on my lap. I can feel their energy, look into their eyes, hear them talk, know what they want, and see what they do. Because I know what to look for, things that are unique to Indigo and Crystal children, I can estimate the percent of children having advanced DNA. I have two friends who also are aware of these special children and spend time with a large

Shumann Resonance currently = Average 7.83 Hz

EARTH'S ASCENSION – NIBIRU AND THE SPIRIT REALM 29

number of children. In talking with them they are coming up with the same or higher percentages than I am.

Based on findings in paleontology this rate of change in human DNA is unprecedented in the history of our planet and it goes way beyond what the theory of evolution would predict. Why is this sudden change in human DNA occurring now and how it is it being done? The ascension plan could not be carried out with humanity's consciousness in the middle of the third dimension.

The collective human consciousness needed to be at least in the fourth dimension with 7% or more of people on the ascension path according to Owen Waters. Because timing was crucial (was a fixed time of entering the photon belt and the Aquarian age) and people at their current rate of growth would not be ready in time, the solution decided on was to invite higher-dimensional beings who have more advanced DNA to come to Earth, take on a human body and help in the ascension.

Their coming with advanced DNA and a higher consciousness would help make humanity ready in time for ascension to happen. Also, they would be invited to stay and help in creating the new fifth-dimensional institutions. These guest humans have had a number of human life times to adjust and prepare. They are now being born in vast numbers, thus the large increase in the number of children being born with advanced DNA

In 1987 there was another sign that the ascension had begun and was progressing. This involves the ascension of the planet itself. Ever since 1942 scientists have been able to measure and record the electromagnetic field generated by Earth. It's referred to as the Schumann resonances. For the first 45 years they kept track of it, the frequency was steady at 7.8Hz. In 1987 for the first time it went above 8Hz and since then it has continued to erratically increase. In February 2017, for three consecutive days, the Human resonance hit 33Hz. Later that year in May it peaked at 76Hz. This electromagnetic energy is

The magnetic field protects planet from solar radiation + is 9% weaker in last 200 years. Hole in field-

recorded every 10 minutes by Russia and the USA and published daily.

There is no scientific explanation for what is causing the increase in frequency, but obviously something has changed to create such a large increase. To me it is highly probable this increase is being brought about by the higher frequency of the photon belt that Earth is moving into and the higher frequency Aquarian energy that we are more than halfway into. The waves of higher frequency being sent to Earth would also be a factor. These three sources of higher frequencies are not only impacting Earth but also helping to raise the collective consciousness of humanity. The fact is that Earth's frequency is increasing, and usual scientific methods are not reveling the reason, or they do not want to talk about why it is happening.

Another reason Earth's frequency has increased is because Earth herself is a living conscious being and she is desiring and ready to ascend. She is a conscious being and has a soul. This soul has a name and it is Santa Kumara according to channeled sources. Though her body was third-dimensional, her soul is at a much higher dimension. By raising her frequency, she is preparing herself for the ascension of her body, the Earth. To house the fifth-dimensional level of consciousness that we are becoming and the fifth-dimensional beings that are now coming to Earth, she needs a fifth-dimensional physical Earth body. Based on numerous channelings both that I have read and that I have been personally given, Earth is now functioning at the very low end of the fifth dimension. She is already ready for what is coming.

This is good news and explains some of the challenges we as a human race and individually are going through. The collective human consciousness at the date of this writing— again based on personal channeled information—is at 4.0. Our bodies are made out of the material of Earth and if Earth is at a different frequency than our bodies this disharmony creates stress in our physical, mental and emotional bodies. This can result in physical discomfort and illness, creating mental illness and emotional problems. The greater the difference in frequency the greater the stress, so it behooves us to make a conscious effort to keep ourselves close to Earth's frequency or higher. If our frequency is higher it is helping Earth and the human race to attain a higher level of consciousness themselves and makes our transition to higher frequencies and consciousness easier.

We have already talked about four of the events happening in space that are assisting in the ascension of not only Earth but the human consciousness, the photon belt, the Aquarian age, the waves of high-frequency energy coming from various star systems and the moving more fully into the higher frequency Aquarian energy.

There is yet another major event that is already beginning to happen that is in space, and that is Nibiru. This will be dealt with in its own chapter. In addition to those there are other factors in space that are also playing a role. Earth is always in motion, it rotates around the sun, while the sun and solar system are rotating around the galaxy, while the galaxy is rotating around the universe, while the universe is rotating around the super universe.

Thus, Earth is always moving into new fields of energy each with its unique frequency. We know also from zodiacs carbon dated as far back as 16,000 to 18,000 years that are virtually identical to today's zodiac, that Earth goes through a 26,000-year cycle in which she goes through 12 different fields of energy each represented by its own sign. Each field/sign is different in frequency. As already mentioned the Aquarian energy is a higher frequency than the Piscean.

Chapter 4

WHERE ARE WE IN THE ASCENSION PROCESS?

T his is an interesting question and the only way I know how to answer it is from personal experience. Over 25 years ago I was guided to do life script readings and I have done more than 3,000 life readings for people on the ascension path; these people we refer to as light workers. These are the only people that are interested in this kind of reading.

During these readings I ask a number of questions, one of them being "During your awake time how much time are you in the fifth-dimensional level of consciousness, the fourth-dimensional level of consciousness, and the third-dimensional level of consciousness."

I am a dowser and the answers come through the dowsing rods. When I began doing these readings, the percentages were as follows: 10%–12% in the fifth dimension, 50%–55% in the fourth dimension, and 30%–40% in the third dimension. Over these 25 years, the percentages have changed dramatically.

Today the percentages for third and fifth-dimensional levels of consciousness have reversed. Light workers today are in the fifth-dimensional level of consciousness about the same percentage of time as they used to be in the third, 32–42% in the fifth, and 12–19% in the third. The fourth dimension (in which we are changing from the third to the fifth-dimensional consciousness) is about the same – 50%.

The light workers are becoming much more loving, kind, forgiving, considerate, and compassionate and being of service to others. They are less service to self, less judgmental, less critical, less depressed, and less fearful. The time spent in the third-dimensional level of consciousness is less than half by my accounts and the amount of time living at a fifth-dimensional level of consciousness has increased significantly. There has been noticeable change in many of them; more self-confident, happier, more loving, more giving, less focused on the material world, less fearful, more peaceful, significant growth in intuition and psychic abilities, deeper and more frequent meditations and increased ability to communicate with deceased loved one and spirit beings.

Let me ask you a personal question. Have you had any kind of a spiritual awakening experience? If so can you recall how fast were you growing in consciousness prior to your awakening? How fast have you been growing since your awakening? If my experience is any indication, your awakening greatly sped up your rate of growth.

My observations are that awakened people are growing at a much faster rate because they are seeking out people and opportunities that stimulate and challenge them to grow. It also appears that growth in consciousness results in spiritual growth. The common tool they are using is meditation. If you have not had a wake-up call and you feel you are ready, ask for it in prayer or better, in meditation.

To me the indications are that humanity is evolving at an unprecedented rate. The percentage of people awakened to their higher spiritual self has never been larger and these people are growing at a rate faster than the general population. Highly evolved beings are coming into the planet at a rate never before experienced in our recorded history.

This has brought about a rise in the collective human consciousness that has created an environment into which the Crystal children are willing to come in ever increasing numbers. Earth itself has increased its frequency as evidenced by the dramatic increase in the Schumann resonance. This information does not tell us where we are at in the ascension process, but it does indicate the progress we are making and the rate at which we are making it and the direction we in which we are moving.

How Far Do We Have Yet to Go?

Good question. Because this is a process without a fixed destination, how far we have to go cannot be determined. What we can measure is the rate of change and that it is faster than any change in human consciousness/behavior in our recorded history. However, many of us wish we were changing even faster. If it is important to you that you have an idea as to the destination, you might want to consider making it a "level of consciousness"; most importantly your level of consciousness.

When you are acting out of love and not ego the vast majority of time, being forgiving, being sensitive and gladly giving of your time energy and money to those in need, communicating and working with your angels, guides, teachers and higher aspects of yourself, seeking to do what you can do so that others might reach their highest potential, and of course loving, respecting, and enjoying yourself. Those are the signs of your personal ascension. That makes a realistic and measurable goal and as you strive towards it you can see and feel the progress.

You can witness the changes being made in the world, at least in your immediate world, by observing your extended family, neighbors, coworkers, and some of the more common events in your community. Many news sources only share the negative because it is not the norm, it is the exception. The good deeds are not news because they are so ordinary.

In order for the larger changes to occur in the third-dimensional institutions of government, economy, religion, media, etc., need to be redesigned based on love, at-one-ment and empowering all people. The only way this is going to happen is if a large enough portion of humanity chooses the path of raising their level of consciousness. A portion of the human population is already living in the fifth dimension. When this transition begins you will know we are in the final phase of the ascension into the fifth dimension. But note that this will be the low end of the fifth dimension and we get to travel all the way through that dimension to get to the sixth dimension.

The nature of human consciousness is it is not static, it is always either moving to higher dimensions or falling to lower dimensions. Human behavior, and the institutions they build, are simply an indication of the level of consciousness at which they are functioning.

Human consciousness is the bedrock. Out of this will come the standard behavior and social institutions. The changes in the consciousness of the light workers, as indicated by the percentages of time they are spending in the third and fifth dimensions and the rate at which this shift is being made gives us a sense of how fast we are progressing.

In addition, this is shown by the rate of increase in the numbers of Indigo children, and especially Crystal children. What is not completely certain is what percentage of the human population is needed to bring about a major shift. The only percentage I have heard or read, from Owen Waters, is 7% need to be on the ascension path. I feel he gets his information from a high level and have a lot of respect for what he says.

For those acquainted with it, another way the shift in consciousness may occur is "the hundredth monkey." Scientists were studying monkeys that lived on several islands in the south Pacific. Their primary food was sweet potatoes.

One day the scientists, watching through binoculars, noticed a young female on a nearby island take her sweet potato to the stream and rinse the sand off before she ate it. They had never seen this before. A week or so later a second monkey did the same, then a third, fourth, fifth, etc. Shortly thereafter all of the monkeys on all of the islands were rinsing the sand off their potatoes, even those that were on islands where they could not see what the other monkeys were doing. This may be how the collective human consciousness will be raised. All we can say with certainty is that we are progressing in the right direction and traveling at an unprecedented rate of speed.

The Event

This 'event' is mentioned in the numerous channelings that I have received, none of which define exactly what it is. I do not have a definitive answer either, but in my personal meditations have been given some information that I would like to share with you.

The result of this change event will be that the third-dimensional level of consciousness will either be separated from the fifth-dimensional level of consciousness or, like the hundredth monkey, all of humanity will be transformed into fifth-dimensional consciousness. The first possibility means the human race will be separated based on their level of consciousness. In the second possibility all of humanity will rise to the fifth-dimensional level of consciousness on this planet in a short period of time after it is being lived by a certain percentage of people. Please read with discernment, as these may not be the only possibilities.

The first possibility is Earth is on a timeline. This can be pictured as a line that is growing in length, the growth is time and the direction points to where it has been and where it is going - we also as individuals, are on our own timeline. The planets timeline is about to split, that is, we are approaching a

Y. When the planet Earth reaches the Y in the timeline the higher-dimensional Earth and lower-dimensional Earth will separate.

The people on the ascension path along with those living mostly in the fourth and fifth dimensions of consciousness will be on the higher-dimensional Earth. Those living mostly in the third dimension will be on the lower-dimensional Earth. Both will be identical but be at different frequencies and moving in different directions. This doesn't fit in with current thinking in physics, but it does happen in biology.

A fertilized human egg can split and become two eggs. Identical twins are then born whose physical bodies look identical. However, they are not identical in terms of personalities, values, interests, beliefs, and outlook. One common source and identical, but distinctly different beings. So, the third and fifth-dimensional Earth will look exactly alike but be functioning in a different frequency ranges.

We humans will go with the planet on which we would be most comfortable, that is the planet that best allows us to continue functioning at our current level of consciousness and can provide the best environment for continued growth.

The second possibility is based on my 35 years of experience working with souls on the astral plane. Up until five years ago there was only one tunnel of light for people to go through. The tunnel of light is the entrance to Heaven according to the 40 years of research on death and dying and my personal experience. About five years ago there suddenly appeared a second tunnel.

The souls who had just died saw one tunnel, the one that would take them to the heaven appropriate for them based on their level of consciousness. In a meditative state I asked the question, "Why the second tunnel?" They said, "The lower one third of the astral plane and heavenly realm had been moved to another third-dimensional planet that is very Earth-like providing a third-dimensional level and not slated to ascend at this time." You must realize that each inhabited planet has its own astral plane and heavenly realm.

Astral plane souls are people who have died and are no longer living in physical bodies and choose to not go into Heaven we will discuss this in the chapter on "Death and Dying". Several times since the appearance of the second tunnel I have been informed that even more portions of the astral plane and heavenly plane have been moved to this the third-dimensional plane and our Heaven has changed so it can accommodate higher-dimensional souls. I have also been told that some people who are highly evolved are choosing to go to this lower evolved planet as teachers and way-showers.

An event, such as the near passing of Nibiru may provide the event that would take many human lives and some of these beings would go to the heavenly or astral plane of the third-dimensional planet. Most of the people ascending with Earth would be removed from the Earth's surface if Nibiru poses great physical danger, going to either Inner Earth or to the motherships where they would be safe and have the opportunity to raise their consciousness yet higher. We will go deeper into this in a later chapter.

To me how it happens is not as important as that it happens. I do know that it is going to happen more smoothly for those of us who have raised our consciousness and are a way-shower and example for others. And I believe this to be true for all of us.

CHAPTER 5

STEPS TO FIFTH-DIMENSIONAL CONSCIOUSNESS

E arth is a classroom and we are the students. Throughout history this is been a very challenging school with the most basic lesson of physical survival being the first lesson. The second lesson is to develop community so that we can help, support and protect one another. Our third lesson is to learn to live in harmony and balance with Mother Nature, respecting and protecting Earth.

Our fourth lesson is how to live peacefully with each other, respecting other's rights and not trying to take what is rightfully theirs. Our fifth lesson is to raise our consciousness through the third dimension into the fourth dimension, the dimension of transition and then attain a fifth-dimensional level of consciousness. This is currently the highest level of consciousness that can be attained on our beloved, beautiful planet. Of the actions available to assist with these lessons, the three most important are:

1. Daily meditation,

2. Connecting and communicating with your spirit family,

3. Becoming one with your soul.

An unprecedented window of opportunity to move out of our limited third-dimensional level of consciousness into the fifth-dimensional level of consciousness has presented itself. This has never happened at any other time in our recorded 10,000-year history. I cannot urge you strongly enough to give serious consideration to avail yourself of this opportunity. In this one lifetime it is possible to achieve more growth than most of us have likely obtained in our last 10-20 lifetimes. Imagine moving out of this third-dimensional consciousness that is based on fear, limitation and separation and moving into a world of love, at-one-ment and personal empowerment. But how can you do this, what are the steps that must be taken?

Because we are all different, some of us have a more developed mental body while others may have a more developed emotional body, and others still are just caught up in physical survival and fear. We are starting from different levels of consciousness, values and beliefs, and we need growth in different areas. While there is no set path, there are certain basics that must be mastered. The starting point for all however, is *desire*.

What you desire is where your heart and mind are focused, it is where you are directing your conscious energy. This creative energy is most powerful if you are using your total mind, conscious and subconscious together. This can only be done in the alpha state, which can be obtained with meditation. Keeping your focus requires discipline whether you are in the alpha or just working with the conscious mind.

It is strongly recommended that when you are deciding what you want to attract or create, whether it is personal growth or something in the outer world, that you specify, "Only if it is for my highest good." In choosing which desire to focus on, keep in mind the only real place we can grow is within our self. Any outer growth is only illusion and temporary. The parts of us that really grow are our mental body, our emotional body and the soul body. These bodies make up the person that we are, and they are eternal. So how do you grow within?

By far the best and fastest way to grow within is to go within. The conscious part of our mind is very limited in its ability to do this. The subconscious mind is a master at it. But even better is to do it using both your conscious and subconscious minds. This can only be done in the alpha state. There are many ways to get into this state and each has to find the method that works best for them. There are traditional meditation practices, such as yoga, mindfulness, two-way prayer, and the runner's high and a host of other techniques.

Whatever method you use the important thing is that you obtain the alpha state. This is the state just above the sleep state where your conscious mind has slowed from its usual 22 waves per second to 8 to 13 brain waves per second. In the alpha state you are working out of your conscious and subconscious minds together. The conscious mind doesn't click off until it hits seven brain waves per second, then it is asleep. The subconscious part of the mind never sleeps. In the act of falling asleep you naturally go through the alpha state.

In my experience if you are practicing a relaxed meditation it is best to have your spine straight and both feet on the floor. The quickest way to slow the conscious mind while at the same time relaxing your body is to focus your mind on your breath and begin counting each time you exhale. This bores the conscious mind with repetition while keeping it focused. When you inhale feel yourself drawing in peace, relaxation and light. With practice, using this technique people are often in the alpha state in about 20 seconds. What is important is that you choose a technique that works for you.

Once you are in the alpha state there are any number of techniques that you can use and you will have to determine which one is best for you. It is suggested that you experiment and try doing different things in the alpha state to see which brings you the greatest meaning. The overriding reason for sharing this information is to help you not only raise your consciousness, but to increase your abilities to help yourself and others. Also, as you raise your consciousness it helps raise the collective human consciousness. Some of the things you might want to try in the meditative state and while working with your spirit family are the following:

1) Asking questions and listening for the answers that may come in your meditation as a thought, emotion or vision. The answer may come later from a person, situation or an opportunity. It is important to remember the question and be looking for the answer. Too often the answer comes, and we have stopped looking for the answer or even forgotten the question. Be discerning when the answer comes. Sense its energy, is it loving, joyful, does it empower you. These are positive and coming from a high source. If the answer carries negative energy it is coming from ego or a lower source and should probably be ignored. Again, when you request an answer, state that it should be for your highest good.

2) Reach out to sense the presence of beings around you. These will most likely be members of your spirit family and they are usually the ones that answer your questions or arrange for the situation or person that brings the answer. Ask your spirit family for whatever help you might need. One method is to ask them to help you open as wide as possible all of your chakras and energy centers in your physical, mental and emotional bodies, and to raise their frequency to the highest possible level. This will allow you to receive information that carries the higher frequency energy and is coming from a higher level of consciousness. Over time as your consciousness raises and becomes closer to your spirit family level of consciousness, they will want you to become one with them and allow them to become one with you, one will and one consciousness. They will be better able to project their thoughts and energy to and through you. This noticeably increases your level of consciousness, energy, channeling ability and the level of information you are receiving. You will also manifest what

you want more quickly. You are now walking in two worlds, the material and the spirit world. Together they are more than either could be separately.

3) In the meditative state ask your spirit family for help in healing your physical body. See and feel them adding their powerful energy to your energy. Visualize that part of your body that needs help and receiving what it needs. Visualize white blood cells and t-cells; the antibiotics needed to fight off an infection; calcium deposited over the break in the bone; stem cells to rebuild an organ or any part of your body; restricting blood vessels that are feeding tumors, warts or anything you want eliminated from your body. Visualization is the primary language of the subconscious and one of its four primary functions is its awareness and control of everything happening in your physical body except what is determined genetically. Working in the meditative state with your subconscious mind and spirit family you have tremendous power to assist and speed up the healing of your physical body.

4) In the meditative state ask that your heart and mind become one *heartmind*. For a mental person this will help to empower their emotional body, and for an emotional person this will help from overreacting and have a calming effect. It helps you stay balanced and changes your perspective. Instead of looking at people, situations and circumstances from only the perspective of your head or heart, you will now be looking at it from both perspectives, thus reacting in a more balanced way. You may also want to ask for help in balancing your masculine and female energies. To be balanced is important if you are going to live in a fifth-dimensional level of consciousness.

5) In the meditative state, be open both mentally and emotionally. You may be communicated with by thought or feeling. Thoughts and ideas may come in that go beyond your current beliefs and even beyond what your logical conscious mind has ever considered but may resonate with

your heart. Ask that what comes to you be for your highest good and then evaluate what level of consciousness this information is coming from. It may be coming from your ego or from a source higher than you are and seem idealistic. If the information comes carrying negative emotional energy, it signals that it comes from a low source. If it is coming from a higher source is always positive, helpful and often will stretch your mind and your beliefs. When information comes from a source outside of you, it is called channeling and if coming from a higher source it can greatly expand your knowledge and wisdom. Discernment using your heartmind is important. Accept only what you are comfortable with and only if you feel it is for your highest good. If it is coming from a higher level you are not accustomed to, do not discard it but file it away, it may make sense later.

6) Out of body travel, also called astral travel, is most often experienced in the meditative state or dream state. It is wise before you start on an out of body journey, or as soon as you are aware that you are out of your physical body, that you ask your spirit family to protect you by enveloping you in a bubble of white light and to keep it strong throughout the experience. You can go anywhere, inside your physical body, outer space, Inner Earth, another country or continent, even another time period. These trips are visual, and sometimes emotional, so you can see where you are and what is around you and what is happening. You may meet some interesting beings and they may have messages for you. You can ruin a trip if you go into fear, so don't, unless it is a negative experience, and then end it by simply opening your eyes. Out of body experiences can be very informative and take you to places you have never imagined or places you have only dreamed of. Enjoy them and learn from them.

7) You may have visitors in your meditation; they may be deceased loved ones, or one of your masters or ascended master teachers, or even someone who wants to take you on

a trip with them. Sometimes they are complete strangers. Sense the frequency of their energy before you accept their message or go someplace with them. Also keep yourself within a protective bubble of white light. While with them you may ask questions, and one question you might want to ask is "how can I help you?" or "why have you come?"

8) You may ask to develop psychic abilities. The beings you will be asking, and who will provide the help, are usually your spirit family. Before you ask, be sure that you have positive reasons for wanting this ability - reasons that can help you and help others - and that it be for your highest good. These abilities include A) physical, mental, emotional and spiritual healing; B) precognition - the ability to see or sense the future; C) reading auras – seeing and interpreting the light emanating from a person especially around their head.

9) Help beings on the astral plane to move into the heavenly realm when they ask for assistance.

10) Send light or other high frequency energy to individuals, situations, circumstances or events anyplace in the world. This can help diffuse them and bring peace, especially if violence is present or threatened. Ask your spirit family to assist in raising the consciousness so that better decisions and actions might be taken. By doing this you can influence not only human events but also things like the weather, making storms less intense or bringing rain where it is needed.

Meditation plays a crucial role in learning the highest and final lesson this Earth school has to teach. It is the goal of all of the ten items above have been leading to and is more important than any of them. If you choose to work on only one thing this is it—*becoming one with your soul*. Your soul is a microcosm of the universal creator. As in a hologram, if your soul were to be enlarged many times you would end up being one with the universe, which is the body of the creator.

Your life energy is the energy of your soul. Your mental and emotional bodies are the eternal bodies of your eternal soul. Your physical body is the temporary physical vehicle created by your soul so that its mental and emotional bodies can fully experience and express itself in this third-dimensional world of duality, free will, third-dimensional consciousness and dense physical matter.

Our soul chose to be here at this time not only for the experience but also to assist in helping this level of creation on this planet transition to a higher dimension safely. This experience and the knowledge gained from it will then be shared throughout the lower dimensions of the universe. Because our soul has gone through it personally it will be able to assist other similar third-dimensional planets go through their transition safely, thus solving a problem that has plagued the universe for billions of years.

You are your soul and your soul is you. You are one and the same. Your soul and you have been in training for this lifetime's mission on this planet for a long, long time. This is the lifetime we have been waiting for and the window of opportunity for us to do what we have been trained for is now open. We cannot accomplish what we are here to do by ourselves. It is going to require us to consciously be one with our soul, one with our spirit family and one with our worldly light worker family.

Meditation will be vital in order to communicate with them and to obtain our inner guidance. Keeping our consciousness at the highest possible level and our chakras and energy centers wide open is also important. We need to have not only the human race but also the planet itself, its waters and atmosphere, the vegetation and animals in protective and loving light. We need to keep in our heart and know, that even if events on the planet's surface appears negative and destructive, that it is a part of the plan and the end result will be positive. The old lower-dimensional aspects on Earth must be removed before the higher-dimensional aspects can manifest.

Our attention is to not be focused on what is leaving but rather to focus our heart and mind on creating what we desire to have in our fifth dimensional home. What a wonderful opportunity to practice and hone our ability as a creator.

This is the job all light workers have signed on for. The tempo of change is increasing, the Illuminati are almost totally gone, and their minions are losing their power and being arrested. The light workers are coming in with their advanced DNA and their Crystal and Indigo energy in record numbers.

Instabilities are evident in many of our world's governments and economies. The natives are restless. Channeled messages are saying our skies are filled with starships coming from not only our galaxy but the universe and beyond. Many of them are here to protect us and help us rebuild.

The lower levels of Earth's astral plane and heavenly plane have been moved to another third-dimensional Earth-like planet. Higher dimensions have been added to both Heaven and the astral plane. Most all of the backstage work has been done. The stage has been set, the audience is in the auditorium, the orchestra is in the orchestra pit and the actors are in their costumes. Momentarily the curtain will be raised, and the play will begin.

You are one of the actors. You either know or will be given your lines at the appropriate time and you know not only what to say, but how to act. We talked about the play, what will happen, the outcome in the long-term results. After it is over the applause will likely extend throughout the entire universe and universal gratitude will be expressed to us and to Earth.

Most importantly, our universe will be a better place and will be able to evolve more quickly and peacefully because a major negative force has been removed. It also shows what can be accomplished when the angelic realm, the space realm the spirit realm and the physical realm, come together and work as one. They can create miracles and we are so fortunate because from the numerous volunteers we were chosen to be one of actors. I hope you are ready for the excitement, because the play is about to begin, and the curtain is ready to go up!

Chapter 6
NIBIRU

Nibiru is the name of a planet, also called planet X by astronomers. It is reported to pass through our solar system every 3,600 years. Its orbit is much larger than any of the other planets in our solar system and not in the shape of a circle, but rather is very elliptical. The reason for this long elliptical orbit is that Nibiru rotates around both of the suns in our double-star solar system. For most this is new information. Astronomers know that many solar systems in our universe have two suns that rotate around each other with planets rotating around one of the suns. It appears that occasionally there might be a rogue planet that rotates around both suns.

It is becoming more apparent, as our knowledge of space increases, that our solar system also has two suns, because of the gravitational effect this second sun has on nearby celestial bodies. Astronomers are also aware that there is something there that is very large, because its gravity is strong enough that it bends light waves that enter its gravitational field. So, astronomers know that something is there even though they can't see. They can know it is size because of the effect on the celestial bodies in that area and how much light waves are being bent. The estimated size of the object is about the same size as our sun.

The only possible reason they can't see it is because whatever event or condition it takes for the sun to begin radiating heat and light never occurred on this second sun. In other words, the second sun did not get turned on, did not ignite, so it is not emitting heat or light. It is dark. Nibiru's orbit takes it around both of these suns and it is the only planet in our solar system that is doing this. When I say "in our solar system" it is as much a visitor as a member as it comes through our solar system once every 3,600 years.

If this is true, why haven't the astronomers discovered our twin sun and why haven't they found Nibiru? Or if they have found them why haven't they told us about them instead of telling us they are just a myth? These are questions I would like answered.

If the second sun is the same size as the sun we know, how can the astronomers not know about it? It seems that something that large and is relatively close to us should be easy to spot. And how can they not know about a planet that currently is in our solar system that is reported to be four to five times larger than Earth? If they do know about these celestial bodies, or even suspect their presence, why aren't they telling us? Is there some kind of conspiracy and if so what is their purpose of keeping this information secret?

In the following pages possibilities will be given. You are going to have to determine for yourself whether these are possibilities or real answers. However, over the several years I have heard of Nibiru and our second sun additional information has been trickling in and has explained some things that until now has been a mystery. So, I am open to the possibility of the existence of a second unlit sun and Nibiru. I'm hoping you also will read this with an open mind as you come to your own conclusion.

Astronomers for years have suspected there was another planet in our solar system. They referred to it as planet X, but they just do not have enough hard evidence to be absolutely certain of its existence. Rather than risk being wrong it is safer and easier to say nothing. This to me is the most probable reason most of us have not ever heard of planet X/Nibiru or the possibility of a second sun.

The reason astronomers cannot see this second sun is because it is dark and difficult or near impossible to see a dark object against a dark background. If, like the sun we know, the second sun had ignited its presence would've been obvious. But how can you detect a dark celestial body against a dark background? There are only three ways and we have already talked about two of them, the gravitational effect on nearby celestial bodies and the gravitational effect of bending light waves.

The third method is successfully being used to find planets in our galaxy. To date, over 1,000 planets have been found. When a planet passes in front of its star there is a dimming of the light coming from the star. The same would be true if the dark sun passed in front of a star, its light would either be blocked or dimmed thus revealing the existence and location of our dark sun.

This method would only work if an astronomer had a telescope aimed in the right place at the right time. For this to happen an astronomer would have to have a good reason to be aiming at that particular area of space at that particular time and so far this has not happen and telescope time is limited and expensive.

There is one channeled source that indicates the possibility of yet another reason the second sun has not been found. The source says that the second sun is always on the opposite side of the sun from us and thus cannot be seen. This may be a possibility, but I must say I am not comfortable with it, but it may resonate with you.

I have a group of nonphysical beings; I call them my spirit family that I have worked closely with for years. From experience I know that they give me good information, so I asked them about this second sun and they said, "Yes it does exist, and it does not emit light or heat; but it does emit a great deal of energy." I asked for information on this energy and they said, "We are not yet at the level that we could understand it because we've never experienced it or even heard of it. But the sun and the energy it radiates plays an important role in our joint solar system and this part of the galaxy."

This is new information for me and I don't even know what to do with it except file it away. It may have meaning at a later time. This is all of the information that I have been personally given on our second sun.

Based on information that I have received from my spirit family I have to question much of the earlier information that has been channeled from other sources regarding Nibiru. It has been talked about in channeled messages I have read for close to ten years. I am going to share both my channeled information and the other channeled information with you so that you can make your own decision, which is right, or if they are only possibilities. This new information also answers many of the questions that I have. I hope this information can be helpful to you in understanding Nibiru and the role it will be playing in the ascension of Earth and humanity.

This is what my spirit family told me about Nibiru. It is a planet with a 3,600-year elliptical orbit, orbiting around both suns. It is roughly four to five times larger than Earth but is only 8% as dense. This means Nibiru's gravity is only about one third of Earth's gravity. This is the reason that it is able to move through our solar system and not have any noticeable effect on the orbits of the planets. If Nibiru were a normal planet its gravity would affect the orbits of the other planets in our solar system. The fact that this is not happening is one of the reasons the astronomers say that Nibiru is a myth.

The reason Nibiru has such low density and gravity is because it is 83% sixth dimensional. This is also the reason it is nearly invisible. Our five senses do not function any higher than the fifth dimension. The fact that 17% of Nibiru is still in the fifth dimension gives it a little density that we can see. It would appear as a ghost like image, and can be photographed only with digital cameras. The images would be hazy and not have a clear outline. This is exactly how the pictures of Nibiru look that I have seen on the computer. The fact that these images can be photographed at all indicates the reality of Nibiru existence and approximate location.

I was also told that Nibiru is inhabited by beings that live within the planet. Other channeled information indicates that on most inhabited planets the life forms live within the planet not on the surface. Close to 80% of Nibiru's highest life forms are sixth-dimensional beings with almost all of the balance being fifth dimension. These sixth-dimensional beings are in mental contact with the sixth-dimensional beings that live within Inner Earth. What control these beings do have, they are using it to make Nibiru's passing by Earth as safe and positive as possible. Nibiru will pass us going between Earth and Mars. At its closest point to Earth Nibiru will be 93 times further from Earth than the moon. This means that Nibiru's gravity will be about the same as the moon's gravitational pull at its closest point to Earth.

As Nibiru gets closer to Earth volcanic activity and earthquakes will increase. At its closest point volcanic activity will be three to four times what it was in 2017, earthquakes will be two to three times more with average intensity and the number of earthquakes will increase about 50%. When the moon and Nibiru are in alignment, the ocean tides will be double their normal height. Three thousand, Six hundred years ago would be 1,600 BC. This is when Nibiru made its last pass by Earth.

At that time Nibiru was a fourth to fifth-dimensional planet, about the same as Earth today. It had the density, weight and gravity four to five times greater than Earth has today. Over the last 3,600 years Nibiru has gone through much of its own ascension, which raised its frequency and lowered its density, weight and gravity. Nibiru density, weight and gravity today are only 13% of what it was when it's made its last pass by Earth. The effect that Nibiru had on Earth in 1,600 BC was tremendous. There was a lot of destruction, trauma and loss of life.

Some of these events are recorded in the Bible in a story we all know, the story of Noah and the ark. Many indigenous tribes in their legends and in their cave paintings also tell the story. I suspect that many of the predictions in the older channelings are predicated on the effects Nibiru had on Earth the last time it passed, when Earth was a lower-dimensional, and much denser, planet.

Earth changes that will occur this time are:

1. Earth's axis in relation to the sun will be slightly changed. This will result in more landmass in the temperate temperature zones.

2. It will slightly speed up the rotation of Earth making our day about 18 minutes shorter. It has already been reported that Earth has already lost one minute a day.

3. The frequency of Earth's electromagnetic shield, known as the Schumann residents, will increase slightly as well the frequency of the planet itself.

4. The sixth-dimensional consciousness field of the Inner Earth people and beings in Nibiru will help to raise the personal and collective consciousness of the few light workers who choose to stay on Earth during Nibiru's transit.

If Nibiru's passage will create a dangerous situation on Earth, the large majority of people who are on the ascension path will choose to go either into Inner Earth or aboard one of the motherships that have offered to house us until the danger is over. Those who are not on the ascension path will not be evacuated and those that die, their souls will go to the astral plane/heavenly realm most suited for them. Those in Inner Earth and those on the motherships will be given ample opportunities to spend time in the consciousness raising chambers.

When they return to Earth the collective consciousness of humanity on the planet will be 4.5 with many people being in fifth-dimensional consciousness more than half of their waking time. These are all positive changes that will make Earth a better place to live and the human race functioning at a higher level of consciousness.

At the end of my session with my spirit family I ask if this information was more than 90% accurate and they said no, it's about 82%. The reason it is not 100% is that with human free will involved, there are always elements of surprise. Also, the ascension plan is always subject to change as the ascension is a fluid situation. In addition, I may not be asking the right questions. So, don't take everything in a literal fashion. Hopefully this allows you to build an overall picture in your mind of the effects that Nibiru may be having upon us and upon the Earth.

I am happy to say the vast majority of effects are very positive and helpful in terms of Earth and humanity moving into a higher-dimensional level of consciousness. I also asked if they could give me an approximate date. I normally would not do this because usually dates given in channeling are not accurate. The reason being that higher-dimensional beings do not live in a linear time, but rather in *now* time. They have no experience with linear time, but when they do hazard a guess it always takes longer than they said. But nonetheless they gave me a day that I will share with you but do not be surprised if it is not correct. The date is May 2020 as the time that Nibiru would be making its closest pass to Earth. In comparison, some Russian astronomers recently stated they are expecting the date to be February 2020.

This new information given by my spirit family eliminates much of the concern about the government keeping secrets from us, or being involved in a conspiracy. Science and the government at this point simply do not have the ability or the technology to clearly detect the presence of Nibiru or the second sun. This new information does confirm that Nibiru and the second sun are real. It also dispels the fear created by the old channelings in its predictions of the mass destruction Nibiru's passage would create. Its passage will, in the end, be a positive event for Earth and all of us. To Nibiru and all of its fifth and sixth-dimensional beings, please accept our deepest gratitude for the role you are playing in Earth's and our ascension! *Thank you*!

The second possible scenario as depicted in the channeled information coming from other sources predicts 500–600 feet tidal waves in some places, a great increase in, not only the number but the intensity, of earthquakes and volcanic eruptions, a greater change in the angle of Earth's axis to the sun, Earth's rotation changing so the sun rises in the West and sets in the East. This would all be caused by the very strong gravitational pull of Nibiru. At its closest point to Earth, Nibiru will be only five times further than the moon is from Earth. It makes sense that when Nibiru is this close to Earth, being four to five times larger than Earth, and having the same density as Earth, it will play havoc with everything on the surface of Earth.

The tidal waves or the earthquakes would destroy most man-made structures. There would be so much volcanic ash in the air that much of the sunlight would be blocked out. This could bring about a new Ice Age. Vegetation would be seriously damaged creating a food shortage. With any warning at all people would be fleeing the coastal areas moving inland. Fifty percent of Earth's population lives within 50 miles of a coastline. All social institutions, governments, healthcare, transportation facilities, etc., would be overwhelmed. A sizable portion of humanity would die. The only bright spot in this picture is, if true, those who were on the ascension path would be removed from the surface of Earth and the danger, being safely housed in Inner Earth or above the motherships.

If there is a choice between these two scenarios, I think it is obvious which one we would all choose. Both of these are speculation, not fact, and possibilities not certainties. It is suggested that in a meditative state you go within and ask your spirit family if either of these are true. Also ask if you are on the ascension path and if there is danger on Earth, are you going to be guided to a place of safety. You may ask these or any other questions of them for yourself or your family and keep your heart and mind open to receive the answers. Request that the answers come from the highest possible sources. I would also suggest you ask that all that happens be for your highest good and the highest good of all that you love. We know changes are happening at an ever-increasing rate and we cannot avoid them. But we can choose to work for the light (ascension) or not. Choose wisely.

In an earlier chapter we discussed *how* the ascension might occur. One of the possibilities was a Y in the time line Earth and humanity are on. It was mentioned that the split in the time line could come with the passage of Nibiru. If a split in the time line is the method that has been chosen it then seemed to me that Nibiru's passage would be a natural time for Earth's ascension to occur. It could be the "Event" numerous channelings have mentioned. It can certainly be said that we live in interesting times, with many possibilities, potentials, challenges and opportunities.

Anyone still bored?

CHAPTER 7

WHAT IT MEANS TO BE A HUMAN BEING

hen people see themselves in a mirror, they may believe that they are seeing who they are. From my perspective this is only partially true. What they are seeing is the outer physical surface of their physical body. They are not seeing anything that is going on within their body, such as their heart beating, lungs breathing, or the blood flowing. Nor are they seeing their thoughts, emotions, beliefs, mind or their divine soul.

In other words, they are not seeing the real person, the person they truly are, only the outer surface of their physical body. We are far more than that. From my perspective we have four major aspects that make us who and what we are. I'm going to refer to these aspects as bodies. All human beings have four bodies. Only one is physical and it houses the other three nonphysical bodies. The essence of who we are exists in the three nonphysical bodies.

In order for the three nonphysical bodies to fully experience and express themselves in this physical environment they need a vehicle made out of the elements and energy of this planet, and that is our physical body. The nonphysical bodies are made of a different energy than the physical body. They are made of higher frequency etheric energy that is not visible to any of our five senses.

Physicists tell us that all matter is made out of energy. Our physical body and virtually everything that the five senses perceive are made out of electro-magnetic energy. Our five senses are tuned to be aware of the ways this energy manifests itself as physical matter, as sounds, lights, gases and liquids. Because our nonphysical bodies are not made of any of these substances they are not detectable by our five body senses. For all intents and purposes our 'other' bodies are invisible to our physical eyes. So, what are these three invisible bodies?

Our second body is our mental body. It deals primarily with thought and it has three components. They are the conscious mind, the subconscious mind and super conscious mind. These will be discussed in detail shortly.

Our third body is our emotional body. It deals primarily with feelings. Many feelings are the result of thoughts. Feelings, when joined together with thought, greatly energize and empower the thought. This is especially true of positive thoughts.

The fourth body is our spiritual body. It is better known as our soul. Let's look further into these four bodies and of the role they play in making us the person we are.

The Physical Body

The physical body is made out of electromagnetic energy and material of Earth: gases, water and minerals. In order to fully experience and function on any of the eleven levels (dimensions or densities) that the astrophysicists have mathematically proven make up our universe, you have to have a host body made out of the energy and materials of that dimension. Thus, a physical body is required to fully function and experience on this third, fourth and fifth-dimensional physical planet. Our physical body is the vessel/vehicle that houses our nonphysical mental, emotional, spiritual bodies.

The physical body provides us with mobility and our five senses, so we can fully experience, understand and interact with Earth and all that is on it. Our five senses in our physical body allow us to only experience dimensions one through five. Dimensions one and two encompass the gaseous, mineral, vegetation, and animal kingdoms. Historically humans have functioned mostly in the third dimension.

As we grow in consciousness it also allows us to experience the fourth and fifth dimensions. Dimensions, six through eleven are beyond the range of our five senses. Scientists refer to them as "dark matter" and "dark energy." In order to consciously experience dimensions six through eleven, we would have to have a host body made out of the energy and materials of those dimensions. This is the only way we can understand and fully experience any level of creation. (Note, some higher dimensions can be experienced in dreams and while astral traveling out of our physical body)

Earth, which until recently has been a third-dimensional planet. In 1987 Earth gradually began increasing its frequency and in 2012 it crossed the line into the fourth dimension. It has now moved through the fourth dimension and has entered the fifth dimension. These higher frequencies are affecting all of our bodies. It is an open invitation to our mental and emotional bodies to move into higher frequencies of thoughts and emotions. Our soul body, which holds our deepest held beliefs, may be reexamining those beliefs. This is an unprecedented opportunity to move from the third-dimensional level of consciousness and physical reality into the fourth and fifth dimensions.

My spirit family told me that the collective human consciousness has moved from the third-dimensional consciousness into the lowest level of the fourth dimension during the 2017 holiday season. The increasing frequencies are causing what are referred to as "ascension symptoms" in our physical body.

The more sensitive you are the more the discomfort you may feel. They include headaches, aches and pains, lack of energy, mild depression, sudden spurts of energy and other unexplained physical symptoms. These are brought about because our physical body has to adjust to the higher frequency energy.

The rate of change is increasing as more and more people awaken to the opportunity to ascend. The awakened ones and those in the process of awakening are called light workers. Presently, the awakened are functioning 30% to 40% of their awake time in the fifth dimension, twelve to nineteen percent of their time in the third dimension, and about 50% of their awake time in fourth dimension, the dimension of transition.

Many people in the lower third-dimensional level of consciousness, who either are not growing in consciousness or growing very slowly, are becoming more disharmonious with Earth. This will increase their physical discomfort and stress.

Because our physical bodies are made out of Earth material, they have a limited lifetime, usually 50 to 100 years. The three nonphysical bodies do not have such a limit. The mental, emotional, and the soul bodies are eternal. Together they are called the astral body and when they leave the physical body, the physical body dies because it has no life force energy of its own. All life force energy comes from the soul. We will go into this in further detail in the chapter dealing with death.

The Mental Body

The mental body is also referred to as our mind. Although the mind is connected with the brain, they are not the same. Our brain is like a computer. It has a lot of information and a lot of abilities, but if it wants additional information, information it does not possess, it needs to connect to sources outside of itself just as the computer via the Internet connects to the cloud. The cloud contains most all of the information stored on most computers around the world.

Our super conscious mind is the cloud, our subconscious mind is the Internet that connects our conscious mind to the cloud, our conscious mind, or brain is the computer. In other words, it is our subconscious that connects us with the cloud, which is the higher frequencies (higher dimensions). The conscious part of our mind is the part that is in contact with the "outer physical world."

During our awakened time our conscious mind is being bombarded with information coming in through the five senses, the eyes, the ears, the nose, the mouth, and the touch. It is functioning at about 20 to 22 brain waves per second, too busy for it to be good at tuning in to the higher frequencies. It is too focused on the outer physical world to have time or interest to look within. It tends to be very logical, good at solving problems, making decisions, planning and taking action. It is certainly an important and essential part for us experiencing, expressing and understanding this physical world in which we live.

Please note that the conscious mind constitutes only 10% to 15% of our mind, while the subconscious, including the super conscious, are 85% to 90%. The super conscious mind may be described as the mind of the soul. It can understand and deal with the higher frequencies and the spiritual information that is beyond the conscious mind.

While our busy conscious mind is running at 20 to 22 brain waves per second it is completely unaware of the subconscious and what it is doing. It does not begin to become aware until our brain waves slow down and reach thirteen brain waves per second. From thirteen to eight brain waves per second we are in what is called the alpha state, a state of 'genius' in which both the conscious and subconscious minds are active and working together and we can utilize close to 100% of our mental capacity.

The slower our brain waves become, the more the subconscious has surfaced and the slower the conscious mind is functioning. At seven brain waves per second the conscious mind clicks off and we are asleep. We are then functioning solely out of our subconscious mind, which does not sleep or ever turn off. During our sleep time the subconscious mind is quite active. Some of this activity we may remember as dreams. We usually remember only the dream we were having as we were waking up and it only stays in our conscious mind for moments after we wake up.

Dreams are often difficult for our logical conscious mind to understand. Part of the reason is the subconscious uses a different primary language than our conscious mind. When we are awake the conscious part of our mind's primary language is words. The primary language of the subconscious mind is visualization.

To interpret your dreams, it is best to be in the alpha state where you are working out of conscious and subconscious together. In that state ask your subconscious about one thing at a time, a person, events or objects that were in the dream to get a clear answer. In this process monitor your feelings as the fuller meaning of the dream may be emotionally based.

There are many things you can do in the alpha state that you either cannot do in the beta state, the normal awake state, or can do faster and better. Intuition is heightened, and most psychic gifts/abilities occur in the alpha state. Astral travel, channeling, psychic healing, healing yourself, controlling your body functions, exploring past lives, precognition, communicating with your spirit family and connecting with your soul are samples of what you can do while in the alpha state.

Please note the alpha state has many names. Some of these names are meditation, mindfulness, the runner's high, two-way prayer, Lamaze birth method, and hypnosis. The alpha state is something we naturally all go through twice a day, falling asleep and waking up. In fact, any time we are in a comfortable position, relax our muscles and clear or focus our mind we often go into the alpha state.

Let's now look at the four primary functions of the subconscious mind.

1) Memory. The conscious mind has a lot of information, but its memory capacity is limited far more so than the subconscious mind. As good as the conscious mind is at remembering events, names, places, directions, etc., it pales in comparison to the subconscious mind's capacity.

The subconscious records everything you have ever experienced, whether you have seen it, heard it, smelled it, tasted it, touched it, thought it, or emotionally felt it. It is all permanently recorded in the subconscious. We know this because under deep hypnosis, which taps into a deep level of the subconscious, total recall is possible. Hypnotists have demonstrated this for decades. The fact is that the subconscious mind records everything and retains it throughout our lifetime and beyond.

Because our mind is not a part of the physical brain it is not impacted by Alzheimer's, dementia, or death. So the information is never lost. This also allows the subconscious mind to accumulate a vast amount of information, knowledge and wisdom, even over many lifetimes.

How can we access the information that we want in the subconscious? We need to go into the alpha state. To do this two things are necessary. The muscles in the body need to relax and the conscious mind needs to slow down. Start by being in a comfortable position with your back straight and feet on the floor in an environment that is either quiet or with soft music. The quickest and easiest way that I have found to quiet the mind is to "bore it" with repetition. Focusing on your breath can do that.

Begin counting each time you exhale. Visualize the muscles in your body relaxing, feel them relax; feel the tension going out from your entire body with your breath. As you inhale visualize you are inhaling light and peace. The light and peace are filling your entire physical body. With each breath you will feel yourself sinking deeper into a peaceful relaxed state. Continue this until you are just above the sleep state.

If you want to test whether or not you are in the alpha state, try to raise a finger. If it comes right up, you are not in the alpha state yet. If you don't want to raise the finger, but you do it anyway, it will not come up smoothly but rather jerkily, you are in the alpha state. (If you are one who feels you cannot meditate we have CDs that can help. Our email address is at the front of the book).

But there is also a downside to this infallible memory of the subconscious. When we were children we were very impressionable and like a sponge we absorbed much of what was around us particularly that which was emanating from authority figures in our life, such as parents and teachers, as well as siblings and our playmates. Not all of these messages were positive or helpful, but in fact some were hurtful, limiting, and perhaps just plain wrong. We were given instructions regarding behaviors, right and wrong, the social customs, proper attitudes, religious beliefs, and self-image (such as: "You are useless. You'll never amount to anything").

The more these messages were repeated the deeper they became ingrained in our subconscious. If we have ignored them and not dealt with the negative messages they are still in our subconscious influencing us still today, helping make us the person we are. This process continues throughout our lives. There are many events and experiences that have shaped us in ways that with which we are no longer satisfied, especially if we are ascending to a higher level of consciousness.

We can change these beliefs, behaviors, and values more quickly and effectively utilizing our subconscious mind in the alpha state. In that state we are very impressionable and each new positive, constructive suggestion we give our self is going directly into the conscious and subconscious together and equals about 100 statements made in conscious beta state.

This means we can affect change in our life in a matter of weeks or several months using repetition in the alpha state that could take years to accomplish with traditional therapy. We can remove limitations, change behaviors (smoking, drinking, drugs, fears, negative judgmental thinking, depression), and whatever else we choose to change. We have the opportunity to remake our self into the person we now truly want to be.

In order for us to effectively work in the alpha state there are a couple of criteria that need to be met. First, we need to totally believe the message that we are giving our self. Second, we need to feel worthy of having what we are asking for and be open to receive it and embrace it when it manifests. It then becomes a part of us. Third, we will likely have to repeat the message more than once, perhaps daily for a week, a month or even slightly longer until it has completely overpowered the old message it is replacing. Fourth, visualize this change within yourself and send it positive emotion, gratitude, joy, and love, thus allowing you to embrace it fully and completely.

Positive emotion multiplies the power of thought many times and, working together with visualizations, can be a most powerful force in your life. Now let's look at the second function of your subconscious mind.

2) Your Physical Body. Your subconscious mind is aware of everything happening in the physical body at all times, controlling almost everything that is not genetically controlled (it can however in many instances influence what is genetically controlled).

Because everything has consciousness, in the alpha state you can instruct your subconscious mind to do what you want done, or stopped being done, to the cells and organs in your physical body. You can take much greater control and responsibility over your health, strengthen your immune system, avoiding illness and disease, and speed up healing.

There are limitations to what you can do with your subconscious mind. Prior to conception while we were still in

Heaven after we decided we were ready for another physical lifetime, we spent 20-25 years planning this life. Working with our spirit family we made a list of what we wanted to learn and the services we wanted to give. We planned the major events, situations, circumstances, arranged for the people and the roles they would play, agreed to play certain roles in the lives of others, etc.

A major role our spirit plays is to try and keep us following our life script, so we will get what we came for. In planning your lifetime, you may have built-in disabilities, limitations, weaknesses, and other challenges. These will give you the experiences that you needed to learn what you came to learn or balance out karma.

Your spirit family may set up the challenges and the opportunities, so you can develop the strengths and abilities you need to do what you planned to accomplish. The greatest limitation is that you must believe that you can do what the situation calls. It helps if you, in your mind's eye, see it successfully completed. This can best be done in the meditative state.

It can also be helpful to know that the primary language of the subconscious mind is not words but visualization, that is, visualizing what it is you want and seeing it completed. By doing this you are building an energetic foundation on which it can manifest and become your physical reality.

You may have to repeat this process as many times as it takes until it is done. You may also ask those working with you in the spirit realm to give you the steps you must take in order to bring your dream into your life or physical reality.

Please understand that what follows is not just coming out of theory; it is coming out of personal experience and the experiences of people I have worked with or friends who have shared their experiences with me.

Personally, working in the alpha state 40 years ago I stopped my hair from falling out. I had to repeat the message/visualization three times about a month apart. I got rid of allergies that I have had since a child. I closed the blood flow to numerous warts, causing them to dry up and fall off. I've also controlled my blood pressure, healed myself of the flu several times, and strengthened my immunization system.

I have a friend who broke her arm, went to the emergency room where a doctor X-rayed it, set it, and put it into a cast. Soon after, she and two friends went into a meditative state and sent healing energy to her arm, visualizing the blood carrying calcium and depositing it over the break, and visualizing the bone being completely healed. They did this for an hour or so until they felt that the healing was complete. To be sure that it was healed they went back to the hospital to have it X-rayed again.

The doctor did not believe that it was possible to heal the bone through meditation. To prove his position, he X-rayed the arm again. The X-ray showed that, indeed, the bone had healed fully.

As I said it is not just theory, it works. Working with your subconscious mind in the alpha state and connecting to your spirit family, you can perform miracles not only on yourself but in healing others, diffusing situations, improving your life and helping to create a better world for us all.

3) Communicate with the Spirit Realm. The spirit realm is the higher frequency, nonphysical part of creation. This realm is rarely accessible with the conscious mind because it does not register with the five physical senses in the physical body. Because logically it cannot exist, therefore to the conscious mind it does not exist, so the conscious mind cannot contact it. It can only be reached through the subconscious mind, and to be consciously aware of what you're connecting with you need to be working in the alpha state.

I've used this state for the last 45 years in much of my counseling and in all of the 3,000-plus people whose life script readings I've done. One of the things I have learned is that all these people have spirit beings looking out for them and working with them. I call them their "spirit family." By spirit beings I mean beings that are not in physical form and are not perceivable by our five senses. Our spirit families often consist of angels, heavenly guides, master teachers, ascended master teachers and higher aspects of our soul. I will explain these beings in a later chapter.

There are several reasons your spirit family is with you. The first is to help keep you on script, to guide you and to assist you when you ask for help. The second reason is your spirit family is with you to learn. *You are their teacher!* They have never been physical or experienced what physical beings experience. By observing and working with you they are learning about these lower dimensions that we are in, and the beings in them, without having to actually go into the dimension.

A third function of your spirit family is to help you. However, "the law of non-interference" restricts them. This is your life and they are not allowed to butt in because they feel sorry for you. They cannot interfere with your life in any way unless you ask. Prayer is one way of asking; be aware that when you pray it is your spirit family that answers the prayer. I prefer talking with my spirit family in the meditative state, as this can be a dialogue whereas prayer is a monologue. I strongly suggest when asking your spirit family for assistance you qualify your request with the statement "if it is in my highest good and the highest good of all it is going to impact."

Your spirit family has a dream for you and for themselves; they would like you to become one with them and allow them to become one with you. Allowing them to be one with you, physically, mentally and emotionally, as you go through all of life's experiences they get to experience more fully than they would just standing on the sideline as a spectator.

In other words, you are their teacher even as they desire to be your teacher and your helper. So, to connect with them and work with them is a win-win situation. Using your subconscious to link up with your spirit family can be a life changing experience and can speed up your growth in consciousness. This is the essence of the ascension process of which we and the planet are in the midst.

4) Creativity. Creativity is the fourth function of your subconscious mind. While the conscious mind is very logical, the subconscious is comfortable thinking outside of the box. This gives it the ability to go beyond the physical realm and into the nonphysical realms. It will consider possibilities and options that the logical mind would reject. This can give some insight into why the logical mind has difficulty understanding and interpreting the meaning of dreams.

Not only are the languages of the logical mind (words) and subconscious mind different (visual) but the subjects the subconscious deals with in dreams are often beyond the scope of logical thinking. If you are confronted with a problem, challenge, or relationship issue, it can be very helpful to go into the alpha state and use both your logical conscious mind and your creative subconscious mind together, coming up with possible solutions.

The creative subconscious will present you with options of which the logical mind would never have thought. You of course, need to use your discernment in picking what you feel is the best way to handle the situation. This can make you more productive, saving time and stress. For those of you that tend to be very logical, it is illogical to restrict yourself to the smaller part of the mind while ignoring the larger part of the mind that has the ability to go beyond the limitations of logic.

In summary, your mind (mental body) is multi-layered, made up of your conscious mind (logical), your subconscious mind (memory, controls physical body, most creative and communicates with the spirit realm) and your super conscious mind (the mind of the soul). Each layer has different abilities. The mental body is more highly developed than it is in any other creature on Earth. It is truly remarkable.

The Emotional Body

The emotional body is a very powerful body. It amplifies many times, both positive and negatively, the power of our thoughts. At any given moment whether we are awake or dreaming it determines how we emotionally feel. The emotional body is what makes us happy, yet it also can make us sad. It can fill us with a sense of dread or hope. It is the emotion of guilt, envy, fear, joy, loneliness, etc. It determines how we are feeling at any given moment. It creates our moods, influencing our thinking and how we respond to other people and situations. It makes our thoughts far more powerful than the thoughts are alone. In other words, the emotional body is influencing us almost all the time.

What triggers our emotional body to feel any particular emotion? There are several triggers, with the most common one being our thoughts. Many thoughts in our English language have emotional components to them. Many words in our English language are used to describe emotional feelings. Most feelings come out of the words we think, read, speak or hear. The emotion can be charged positively or negatively. We can feel this energy in our physical body as well as our mental body. Emotions can thus empower us or rob us of our energy.

This behooves us to develop the self-discipline of consciously being aware at all times of our thoughts and the emotions that they are creating and the effect they have on us. If we train ourselves to be positive thinkers we are going to be happier, more energetic, more productive and better company. Program yourself, and this can best be done in the alpha state. In this state repeatedly tell yourself, "I am always aware of the thought in my mind, if it is negative I will deal with it now or replace it with a positive thought. I am a positive thinker and do not hold onto negative thoughts at inappropriate times." If you are in what you consider a negative situation focus on what you can do to improve the situation. If there is no positive solution available at the present time focus your thoughts on possible positive outcomes.

A big component of depression is a person holding on to negative thoughts. Negative thoughts are downers, nonproductive, depressing, and inhibit us from taking appropriate action. If you are around negative depressed people learn to protect yourself, so they do not pull you down emotionally. To protect yourself ask your spirit family to surround you with a bubble of white light; you may need a double or triple bubble. Ask them to keep you and your bubble filled with their love light, joy and peace, with instructions that your bubble is to deflect or transmute anything directed toward you that is not for your highest good. The only thing that can enter your bubble and you is to be positive and empowering.

To help a depressed person in your presence be uplifting, lighthearted, and help them look at the positive potential outcome instead of the negative outcome they are picturing in their mind. Much negative thinking is playing the game "what if", with a focus on the negative "ifs". Help them explore positive endings. If they are ready to hear, let them know that virtually all that exists is, and continues to be, created out of thought, especially thought empowered by emotion. The very things they are fearful of, and worrying about, they are helping to bring into their life with their thoughts and emotions. They can help create the happy ending by visualizing it and feeling it within themselves. This will also help them feel better in creating a win-win situation. Thankfully, negative emotions are not nearly as powerful as positive emotions. The suggestions given to help overcome depression can also be used to overcome anxiety, and irrational or chronic fear.

I find that the emotional bodies are at a different stages or levels of development in different people. Some people, those we call sensitives, have a highly developed emotional body. They can sense the energy coming from a person, an object, a place and event. My wife, Ortrun, is a sensitive and more emotionally expressive than I am. For her and others alike, it is very important that they are aware of their thoughts and emotions virtually all their awake time. I am so grateful that

Ortrun's nature is to be happy, loving, and outgoing. This allows us to do much of our spiritual work together.

A person with an under developed emotional body is apt to function predominantly out of their mental body. If you watch the TV program the Big Bang Theory the lead character Sheldon could be seen as an example of this type of person. They are challenged in their social interactions; they are uncomfortable with other people expressing emotion, uncomfortable with physical touch, limited in their ability to express positive emotion and may be diagnosed to have autism spectrum disorder (which now includes the previous diagnosis of Asperger Syndrome). They tend to be highly intellectual in their area of interest. They tend to be task and thing oriented and minimize human interaction. Some do not understand and are not comfortable with people who express emotions.

In metaphysical circles this type of person is referred to as Indigo. I think you can understand that it is challenging to be at either end of the emotional spectrum, having too much or not having enough, or any, emotions. I believe both types of people have some contributions to make to the human race and they are all deserving of being accepted, respected and loved. They have chosen a tougher life to live than those who function between the extremes. Later in this book we will look at the primary cause for these extremes in our emotional body, but to give you a hint, now they have come from different places and realms in the universe.

The Spirit Body

This is the third nonphysical body that experiences and expresses through our physical body. This body holds our deepest held beliefs, especially those that are of a religious or spiritual nature. However, this is not the true essence of this body. It is more like the frosting on the cake. The true essence of the spiritual body is the soul. The question now is what is the soul? I was a Lutheran for the first 40 years of my life, and a Lutheran minister for 13 years. I have a master's degree in theology from the Lutheran Theological Seminary at Gettysburg, Pennsylvania, and I don't recall having ever heard about what the soul is.

Christianity, as well as most major world religions, acknowledges that we have a soul, but in much of Christianity they don't dwell on it or define it. So again, what is the soul? I have an answer given to me by my Spirit family in meditation. *The soul is a microcosm of our universal creator.*

Early in this book I talked about the creation and offered you a theory that the creation is made out of conscious energy and that the consciousness in the energy is that of the creator. This, in my mind, makes the universe the body of the creator. It means that the consciousness of the creator is within everyone and everything, so all that is, is the creator experiencing and expressing itself.

This belief is somewhat backed up by quantum physicists who have proven that consciousness is present in photons, a sub atomic particle of light. Light is energy and physics teaches us that everything in the universe is made from energy. Adding to this is the fact that the universe follows the laws of holograms, and an increasing number of astrophysicists are saying the universe may be a hologram.

Holograms are made of pixels of light, and if any pixel of light is enlarged enough it will be the entire hologram. In my mind this makes our soul, like a pixel in hologram of the universe, a microcosm of the consciousness of the Creator within us. To state it a different way, our soul is an aspect the Creator within us. It is from the soul that we get life energy, the energy that allows us and the Creator to fully experience and express through us.

Can you imagine what you and your life would be like if you were fully aware of the divine essence in you and living as *one* with it? The *love, wisdom and power* you would have and what you could do! I believe this is exactly what Jesus did; he became one with his soul, and his soul was then free to express fully though his physical body and performed all of the miracles. When Jesus said, "My father and I are one" he means "I have become one with the divine essence in me", meaning his soul. He then went on to said, "All of the signs and wonders you see me do, these and even greater shall you do." I believe what makes Jesus the Christ is he became *one with his soul* and was trying to show and tell us that we can do it too! I feel this is the highest and final teaching we are to learn in this Earth school.

I find it helpful to begin my day with meditation, a part of which includes communicating with my soul, inviting it to use my physical, mental, emotional and spiritual bodies to experience and express what it desires. I ask that we be one throughout the day, one consciousness, one energy, and one will. I also do the same thing in the evening, as I'm about to go to sleep. I invite my soul to use all that I am during my sleep time that again it might experience and express what it wills.

For me, becoming one with my soul has been a process and continues to be a process that I am still working on. Part of it is overcoming the blockages coming from my Christian background, which stressed, "You are a sinner. You are lost, and you need a savior," along with many negative messages that are disempowering. In my daily meditations I ask my spirit family to help me open wide my chakras and energy center and keep them at the highest possible frequencies. I ask for their guidance and help in becoming one in all ways with my soul.

I am not performing miracles yet, but I feel the day is getting closer. I share this personal part of me to show what you can achieve if you too desire to become one with your soul. The starting point, I believe, is to state your desire, in meditation, to your spirit family and your soul asking them for their guidance and help. Then set up a daily routine that will become a path leading to fulfilling your desire. In doing this you will be helping to fulfill one of the reasons Jesus came here. He tried to tell and show us what our potential is and who we truly are, what we can do and the miracles we can perform.

CHAPTER 8

INDIGO AND CRYSTAL CHILDREN

I am going to be sharing a lot of information with you about these special children and you could wonder where all this information came from. I have been a Santa for the last 14 years and have had over 25,000 children sit on my lap, look into my eyes and tell me what they wanted for Christmas. I feel their energy, their excitement and sense of awe. I have never done anything I enjoy more!

I have been aware of the Indigo and Crystal children for 16-plus years. In feeling their energy, observing their behavior and demeanor I am able to sense the children who are unusual, having advanced DNA. When I began being Santa I could sense 12-15% of the children I saw had the advanced DNA that manifests in children as Indigo and Crystal energy. Today over 60% of the children have this advanced DNA. These percentages come not only from my experience but also from two other people who work with a large number of children.

One in Michigan is a minister, a baseball coach and a Santa. The second for many years has worked in school systems in

Florida helping children as a speech therapist. All three of us have been aware of the Indigo and Crystal children for years and when I see them, we compare notes. I have been amazed when I ask them what percent of children saw last year that carried these energies and their number was the same as mine! This has been going on for over 10 years!

We have also observed in these special children over these years the percentage of Indigo energy has been decreasing and the Crystal energy has been increasing and now is almost double the Indigo energy. In addition to being Santa, I have been a dowser for many years. For 100s of years dowsing has been used to find water, oil and other minerals in the earth, but it also can be used to get answers to yes/no questions. For over twenty years I've used dowsing to check over 3,000 adult's and children's DNA, asking how many active codons, and if they have Indigo/Crystal energies, how much of each.

Being a member of a large family (four siblings, five children, eleven grandchildren, and eleven nieces and nephews) I have long term and in-depth experience with children. And yes, our family has a few of these exceptional children. Beyond this personal experience I have read a number of books, articles and channeled information dealing with the Crystal and Indigo children.

An increasing percentage of children coming into the world have advanced DNA. These children are called a number of different names; star children, rainbow children as well as Indigo and Crystal children. I'm going to refer to them as Indigo and Crystal children because they are coming with two distinctive personality and behavior traits. They were given these names because these are the colors seen in their auras by people who are able to see auras. All of these children have advanced DNA.

DNA looks like a twisted stepladder; the two outside lines twisted in the form of a helix are connected by 64 parallel lines, like the rungs on the ladder. These parallel lines are called codons. DNA is the basic building block of all life forms.

Humans are the most advanced life form on the planet and have more codons than other life forms. Of their 64 codons only 20 are active in normal people. Normal people in this mean people who have come through the evolutionary process and evolved here on Earth; and this is the vast majority of humans at this time.

Geneticists studying human DNA in the past labeled the 44 inactive codons as "junk". In 2007 geneticists were asked to study children that were different, that have come to be known as the Indigo and Crystal children. They found these children had 21 to 24 active codons. When they were given an IQ test most were found to have IQs between 130 and 140, with a few as high as 160. The normal IQ is 90 to 110.

They also exhibited different behavior patterns and abilities, which we will deal with shortly. After studying these unique children, the geneticists did a complete reversal. Instead of referring to inactive codons as junk, they began referring to them as, "our as-yet undeveloped potential." Even though the Indigo and Crystal children had 10% to 20% more active codons than normal people, still only about one third of their human potential is being utilized as they still have 40-plus inactive codons. This leaves a whole lot of room for all of us to grow in our humanity. Now let's look at the unique traits of these special children.

Indigo Children

People who have the ability to see and sense beyond the normal human range first used the name Indigo. They saw the color indigo in the auras of these exceptional children. These highly intelligent children also had some unique behavior and traits. Their mental bodies are highly developed; that is they work very much out of their head, while their emotional bodies are mostly under developed.

They do not understand emotions expressed by other people because they do not feel these emotions themselves. They often seem to lack empathy because their focus is more on themselves than on other people. They seem to lack the ability to understand what other people emotionally are going through. They can be challenged in interpersonal relations and in social situations. They may try to avoid personal interactions because it makes them feel uncomfortable. They may be diagnosed with Asperger's syndrome, which is one of the previously separate sub-types of autism, now folded into autism spectrum disorder.

Those with high amounts of Indigo energy may often present themselves as if they know more than other people. They do not like being told what to do. They can be task and thing oriented. On the positive side, it is the Indigos that have brought us the electronic revolution of computers, cell phones, the Internet, social media, electronic games, digital cameras and high definition TV.

They are the ones that have made the space program successful and are behind most of our technological advances for the last five to six decades. They are technologically creative and innovators. They see possibilities others often miss. Vocationally they work best alone or with other Indigos who have common interests. Nikola Tesla is a classic example of an Indigo person. If you watch the "Big Bang Theory" on television the main character Sheldon is another example.

Historically, it appears to me that a very small percentage of people with Indigo energy, perhaps 1%, have always been here. These were the philosophical, political, military, religious, financial and scientific leaders down through the ages. Leonardo da Vinci and Isaac Newton are examples. What is new is the growing percentage and sheer number of children that are coming into the world with Indigo energy.

These children can be a challenge to raise or educate in a society that is not comfortable with people that are different or do not fit a structured educational system. They may not feel a need to please or cooperate with others. They can bury themselves in their current project blocking out all that is being said or done around them. They often act like they know more than others and do not like being told what to do.

This makes it hard for parents and teachers when they are making suggestions; trying to correct behavior or otherwise attempting to guide or control them. They are generally uncomfortable being touched or touching others. They are happiest and most content doing what they want to do, and this usually involves working on a task, alone, that they are interested in or playing alone with their electronic toys.

Here are some suggestions for parents and teachers from my point of view. Whenever possible avoid telling an Indigo child what to do, rather give them choices. You control the choices, but they feel they are in control because they get to choose. For example, if they have a school assignment that is due on a certain date they can be given the choice of doing it now or cleaning their room and putting everything where it belongs and doing the homework at a later specified time. They do not have a choice about doing the assignment, but they have a choice about when they do it.

Most of these children at any given time have a favorite toy, activity, etc. They can do their homework now or forgo that toy or activity until the homework is complete, their choice. You can also reward them for good behavior. Indigos often have a difficult time understanding the cause and effect relationship. In this way you are teaching them this concept, and this will serve them well in the years ahead.

It is also important to identify their interests and do all that you can to see that they have the opportunities to pursue and develop those interests. If you sense that they are trying to manipulate you, let them know that you understand what they're trying to do; it will usually diminish. Because they are so challenged in the social arena, it is so difficult for them to make friends. It can be very helpful to invite another child they appear to like to come for a sleepover or some other event with just the two of them. If they show an interest in any physical activity, music, sport, etc., encourage and support this especially if it involves being around other people.

Most Indigo children enjoy computers, electronic games and gadgets, cell phones, computer games, remote control vehicles, boats, drones, robots, etc. It is important that you show them that you love them by joining them in activities that they enjoy, playing games that they like, by telling them that you love them, by treating them with food, gifts or activities that you know they would like.

Occasionally these may be used as rewards. Because they tend to be focused on themselves, if they do something for you or someone else praise them and remind them how good it made them feel when they did something good for someone else. They also need you to be their advocate at the school. Because they are different, with their high IQs they learn faster, often lack normal social skills and have different interests, other students may pick on them and teachers may not understand them. They need their parents to stand up for them.

History has shown that most Indigos make positive contributions to society and it is likely all Indigo children in your life will too. Hans Asperger, who had the syndrome named after him, became a pediatrician researching and treating children with the syndrome. Early in his career he became involved in pediatrics in a large hospital in his home country of Austria. Many of his patients went on to become highly successful in their field.

The Asperger syndrome, for insurance reasons, is now lumped in with autisms and some of the Indigo children get this label. Based on what I have read and my own personal experience I feel strongly that the world is a better place because Indigos are here.

The number of children that have Indigo energy without some Crystal energy is very small. The vast majority, in my experience, has both. The behavior traits they have indicate which they have more of. A child with 60% Indigo and 15% Crystal will have more Indigo characteristics, but not as extreme because the Crystal energy gives them some sensitivity and social awareness.

Crystal Children

The Crystal children have highly developed emotional bodies. If they have a large amount – over 70% Crystal energy - they can be very sensitive and intuitive. They operate primarily from their heart. Their IQs tend to be slightly higher than the Indigos. They are very loving, warm and affectionate; they love to cuddle and be touched. They are very sensitive and may sense how other people are feeling, physically and emotionally without being told. The feelings and thoughts of others around them very much affect them.

All five of their senses tend to be more developed than normal. They often see, feel and sense things that others don't. When they are very young, infant to school age, they may have imaginary playmates, but they are only imaginary to us. If you asked them what the imaginary playmate look like, what they're saying, what they're doing, what they're wearing, a child who is 75% Crystal or more can tell you.

They are able to see, hear and feel beyond the normal physical realm. They can see into what we call the spirit realm; angels, deceased grandparents, Devas and other beings that inhabit the spirit realm. Some Crystal children will know what you are thinking, what you are going to say or do before you say or do it. Many would label them as being psychic.

They are also very attracted to animals. It can be important to them to have a pet, a cat, a dog, a canary, or even a goldfish. They have a special love for nature and they seem to be most comfortable when they are close to nature. They are usually happy and joyful children. They can bring much joy and happiness to most any family. If you are sensitive to their energy, if they even walk into the room, they will likely make you smile and pick up your spirits.

This super sensitivity can help them be a most beautiful person, but it also can create challenges. The beings from the spirit realm may not always be positive, nightmares can occur, loud voices can scare them, negative emotions make them want to leave the room, they cannot tolerate fighting, physical violence or arguing. If children at school say something negative about them or what they're wearing it hurts them deeply. Rejection will quickly bring them to tears.

If a child has a large percentage of Crystal energy with no Indigo energy, they can become overwhelmed not only by what they see and feel, not only what is happening in the physical world, but they may also see, feel and sense what is happening in the spirit world around them. If it becomes too much for them they will withdraw into themselves in order to protect themselves and may be diagnosed as being on the autism spectrum. If a child has a lot of Crystal energy and some Indigo energy they be called an empath or simply a sensitive child. Because of their sensitivity, high desire to please, need to be accepted and loved they can be prone to anxiety and depression.

For parents and other people working with Crystal children it is important for you to be aware of their sensitivity and their great desire to please you. As loving as they are they also need a lot of love. Following are some suggestions you might want to consider. It is important that you teach them how to protect themselves. All of us have a group of spirit beings, primarily angels that are with us 24 /7.

Teach Crystal children to ask their angels each morning before they go to school and each evening as they go to bed, to build a strong beautiful bubble of white light around them and to fill them and their bubble with love, peace and joy; and to make the bubble strong enough to keep out everything that is not for their highest good. If they want, they can ask the angels to stay in the bubble with them. They need to believe and know that inside their bubble they are safe and protected. This is only one technique; there are many others available, but this is the one my wife and I use for our self, so we know it is effective.

For parents of Crystal children, a peaceful loving home is very important. They need to know that you love them and support them in all ways and that they are safe. Show them affection and express your appreciation for all that they do. If they have imaginary playmates invite them to talk about them and never tell them it is just their imagination because it is not; it is real for them. Avoid using a loud voice with them or with others when they're present. If you have a disagreement to settle with another family member go into a room and close the door. Do not express strong negative emotion or thoughts in their presence.

Fighting or physical violence of any kind is a no-no if they are around. They need you to be their advocate, their defender. If events are occurring in schools that are hurtful to them, please talk to the teachers or administrators about the problem and what can be done to solve it. If their friends or classmates are hurting them, talk to them, identify their behavior and how it is making your child feel, and ask for their help.

The same holds true for words and actions of siblings and spouses and other family members. If they have nightmares, which can be a sign that something is amiss and needs to be dealt with. If the nightmares, anxiety or depressions persist and you cannot identify and deal with what is wrong, it is important that they get the help they need as soon as possible.

The Crystal energy is the highest energy that humans tend to carry. It is so loving, so joyful, it is so alive and vibrant that even just writing about it brings a smile to my face. I love being with them; they pick up my spirits and make me smile. They call forth the love from within me and whenever I can, I enjoy sharing a hug with them. This is the effect these beautiful children have on me. I'm sure that they have that same effect on anyone who is at all sensitive and open to receiving and giving love. I'm also glad that they're coming in ever-larger numbers because their energy is what I think the world needs and hopefully is now ready for.

In my experience about 95% of children that I see in my role as Santa Claus each year who have advanced DNA carry both Indigo and Crystal energies. Those that have just Indigo or Crystal energy, they and their families, are faced with the challenges just talked about. To work predominately out of your head and not your heart, or to work largely out of your heart and not your head creates imbalance. Those that have both energies have a far better chance of being either balanced or nearly balanced. My experience is that some of the children have about equal amounts of Indigo and Crystal energies, while most will have more of one than the other. This means that they will have more Indigo or Crystal traits but have the ability to function out of both head and heart but not in equal amounts.

The Indigo energy allows those with predominant Crystal energy to function in a technological world. The Crystal energy allows those that are predominantly Indigo to live in a world with people and to get along and even enjoy them. The Crystal energy is relatively new on Earth. When Crystals attempted to come in at earlier times, the fact that they were so sensitive to the hurt and pain around them, and would not fight or defend themselves, often meant that their lives were cut short, so they stopped coming. Now the frequency of Earth and humanity have risen high enough that the Crystal children can exist here and help raise the consciousness of humanity to the fifth dimension with their joy, love and desire to serve. The balance between Indigo and Crystal energies has changed. Children with both energies tended to have more Indigo than Crystal energy, but over the last several years it has shifted. More children are carrying more Crystal energy than Indigo.

Our educational system is failing these highly intelligent special children. Teachers are teaching to the test, not to the children. With the special children being more intelligent they learn faster, and in normal schools, where they teach to the average child, the Indigo children get bored, they are not noted for their patience, and are apt to act up, disrupting the class. Some charter schools have been created to deal with these special children, especially the Indigos, but there are far more of these children than there are schools to teach them. Our educational system needs to be updated so that the interests and potential of each student can be more fully developed.

Crystal children, with their desire to please, can do okay in most public schools, but the Indigo will be challenged. An ideal school for Indigo will be structured around student's interests, not grade levels based on age. The desire to learn is high if the subject is something the child/person wants to know. How marvelous it would if a student could choose to be part of a group studying what they are interested in, such as computers, electronics, wood working, mathematics, social studies, art, music, outer space, rockets, cars, literature, etc. In each interest area, older more advanced students would be encouraged to help younger students and may even take on mentoring another student. This would build self-esteem and more individual attention would be given where needed. This also frees up the teachers to devote their time to where it is most needed. Projects would be encouraged for both individual students and group projects in their interest areas. Another option is, each school day for one or two periods the students would gather in interest groups, with two or three grade levels working together on a commonly agreed-upon project. The chances are if they want to make progress the students are going to have to know reading, writing, and math. By using the students interest to motivate them to learn can be of powerful tool especially for the Indigo children.

Interest-centered learning not only facilitates the learning process, but it also encourages developing social skills such as communication, negotiation and just plain working together with other people. This could be most helpful especially for the Indigo children and it would put them in close proximity to some who have Crystal energies, so they could learn how to appropriately express feelings. It could lessen the boredom and disruptive behavior. These are just a couple of ideas of how schools could be more helpful to these advanced special beautiful people that are now coming in mass numbers into our lives and communities. If you have children, seek out the school that is best suited for them.

Evolution is not a straight-line angling slightly upward. Anthropologist are now saying evolution appears to be more like a staircase where not much happens over a long period of time and then suddenly there is a jump upward, and new species appear. Today new species are reported almost monthly in National Geographic and Discover magazines. With the sudden change in human DNA and sudden appearance of so many new life forms, it is my belief that we are on the vertical part of the staircase, not the horizontal. Not only are life forms changing, but Earth is also changing rapidly as evidenced by the rapid increase in the frequency of the Schumann frequency of Earth and the multitude of other changes all occurring simultaneously. This can't be just a coincidence; there has to be a plan behind it. All these events point to a rapidly ascending Earth and humanity.

These advanced children with their high IQs, their open hearts, their technical skills, their caring and concern for others are here at this time to assist not only in the ascension process of the human race and Earth, but also in rebuilding human society, including religions, economies, governments, education systems, healthcare systems and all other institutions of society. The plan, as I understand it, is that they will build on the level of love and not fear, the level of at-one-ment and not separation, and the level of empowering each and every person, giving them the opportunity to maximize their potential.

You are blessed if you have one or more of the special children in your life. Know that the only way this could occur is if you yourself were well qualified to be their parent, grandparent, teacher or friend. If you need help in your role, it is available if you ask, not only from schools, churches and other social institutions, but also from the spirit beings over lighting you and the spirit beings over lighting your special child.

Do not hesitate to ask as they are not allowed to interfere and thus cannot help without your asking. You have a special responsibility in helping this child to maximize their potential in whatever area that might lie, and to help them build the self-confidence to do what they're here to do. But above all these children need to know that you love them and will do anything in the world that it takes to support them.

You also might be interested to know, in my experience, the special children tend to come into the lives of people who also have advanced DNA themselves that manifest as Indigo and Crystal energies. Usually your children simply have more of these energies than you.

Before we end this topic, I want to address a question I am often asked. "If my child is 48% Crystal and 19% Indigo what is the rest?" The rest is normal human. I feel we are indeed blessed that so many children are coming into the world with these wonderful abilities. If they continue coming into the world at the rate they are now, in a couple of generations they will make up the majority of the human race. Those that are already here have helped raise the collective consciousness of humanity. Their coming gives hope for a much better future for all humanity.

In order to understand what death is, it would be helpful to have a quick review of who we are as a human being. This is covered in the earlier chapter "What It Means to Be Human". We are not just a physical body; we have a physical body made of earth material so that we can fully experience and express ourselves in this physical environment. Our physical body houses the person that we truly are. We are a mind that connects to our physical body through our brain. We are emotion and feeling. And we are a soul that is a small part of the consciousness of our universal Creator. Each of these four aspects will be referred to as bodies; thus, we each have four bodies.

The physical body is the only one that has an expiration date. The mental, emotional and soul bodies are eternal and together are referred to as our *astral body*. When the astral body leaves the physical body, the physical body dies. It does not have life force energy of its own. Life force energy comes from the soul that is a part of the astral body. This explains why the brain and heart both flat-line at the same time.

There is no medical/biological reason for this to happen. The brain has enough oxygen and nutrition to last for three to five minutes after the heart stops beating without incurring permanent brain damage. Electrical activity ends when the heart stops beating and that is because when the astral body leaves there is no life energy in the brain or the physical body.

We are going to look at death from two different perspectives. One perspective is that of the person who has died. The second perspective is that of the person who was lost a friend or loved one. Let's begin by looking at death from the perspective of the person who has died. Some would say that this is not possible because how can we know. Based on research that has been done over the last 50 years on death and dying and combined with 35 years of personal experience of working with people after they have died, provides a good amount of information to work with.

Research was begun in the 1970s by a psychologist named Elizabeth Kubler Ross and has continued ever since. The research focuses on people who have had what is called a "near-death experience". This is an event where the physical body is dead with no heartbeat and no electrical activity in the brain. This is the medical definition of death. If this happens in the hospital a medical team immediately goes to work trying to resuscitate, that is, to bring the person back to life. If they are successful within the three to five minute window the person does come back to life with no brain damage.

What is fascinating in this research is that roughly 30% of people who are resuscitated remember what happened while their physical body was dead. This is evidence that life continues after the physical body dies. What is even more intriguing is that the vast majority of these people had the same experience while their physical body was dead. This gives us insight into what happens immediately after the physical body dies. All of this is convincing proof that our consciousness does not die when the physical body dies. There is life that continues and exists without a physical body.

This is the experience they reported. They rose out of their body, ascended up near the ceiling and hovered there for a brief period of time during which they could see and hear everything that is going on in the room. They could see their physical body lying there with people working on it and did not feel any desire to go back into their body.

They then felt like they were moving rapidly through space; it was dark all around except in the distance ahead of them was a white light that they felt attracted to. When they got to it, it was a tunnel of light. They intuitively knew if they went into the tunnel their lifetime was over. They all reported their thoughts went to their family; were they really ready to leave them; to their dreams that they had not yet realized; to their goals that they wanted yet to accomplish.

In other words, their focus was still on their physical life and because this was not their final exit point they immediately found themselves back in their physical body. Their heart started beating and electrical activity returned to the brain and they suffered no physical damage.

Many said they had changed emotionally. They had lost all fear of dying and saw their life in a different light and they were more peaceful. Their values had shifted and no longer got upset over unimportant issues. Overall, they were happier and the quality of their life and relationships improved.

We do not have empirical research on people who died and are not resuscitated. Here we draw on the experiences of people who feel loved ones that have died and spirit doulas have contacted them who work with people after they have died. I am and have been a "spirit doula" for 35 years working with souls who chose not to go into the heavenly realm when they died, but now have changed their mind.

They do not know where the tunnel of light is and they come to me for help and I am able to help them. People that we call psychics will often have clients ask them to a contact loved ones who are on the other side, that is dead. They are often successful in doing this and what they tell their client is often spoken in words and phrases that the deceased would use. This way authenticates the contact and the message.

There is scientific evidence, though not directly relating to life after death, which speaks to the probability of life after death. As stated elsewhere in this book, many quantum physicists believe that everything that exists in the universe has consciousness. Thus, the consciousness can exist without a physical body. The 40 years of research on death and dying gives us clear evidence that consciousness does not die when the physical body dies.

This research has also determined that at the instant of death the physical body loses 5/8 of one ounce. This knowledge was learned with the permission of the people who were dying. They were hooked up to EKG and EEG machines measuring heart and brain activity. They and their hospital bed were put on very sensitive scales. At the same instant the monitors flat lined, that is the heart and brain stopped functioning, the scale moved showing a weight loss of 5/8 of one ounce. This is then assumed to be the weight of the astral body.

Astrophysicists tell us that they have mathematically proven that the universe has 11 different dimensions or levels. With our five bodily senses we can only be aware of the lower five dimensions; the sixth dimension and higher are functioning at vibratory rates higher than our five senses function. This allows for the possibility that there could be a higher-dimensional place, some call it Heaven that can exist without our five senses and logical mind being aware of it. Science does not prove that there is an afterlife, but it does indicate that it is entirely possible.

The belief in life after death has been a part of our written history from the beginning of our recorded history, and oral tradition carries this belief back even further in time. All religions throughout history talk about and attempt to describe what the afterlife is like. It's only in more recent years with the advent of technology and modern science, both of which come out of the logical conscious mind, that life after death has been questioned.

In more modern times, since the invention of the camera, especially digital cameras, there have been innumerable pictures taken of ghost-like beings. With the advent of cell phones with built-in digital cameras the number of "ghost pictures" has dramatically increased. In the numerous funerals I've had over the years, I share my experience that the recently departed loved one may attempt to contact them. I tell them of my interest and study in life after death and if they feel they have been contacted to please share it with me. Many have told me that they feel their loved one's presence and that love or even thoughts are being exchanged.

In a time of crisis something pops into their mind that was a common saying of their loved one that is calming, and they feel their presence. They may also hear their loved one's voice inside their head or sometimes even spoken out loud. Some have reported dreams in which deceased visited them loved ones. A few have not only seen and talked to them but have been touched by departed family members.

What I've learned from this is that the death does not separate us completely from our loved ones. They continue to be aware of our life situations and of us, and they also desire to reach out not only to help us, but also to let us know that they are okay. The death of the physical body does not sever the bonds of love; it somewhat limits and alters how that love is expressed and experienced. If you've lost a loved one this can hopefully bring you comfort and peace.

If you've lost a loved one, it is natural to feel grief, sadness, sorrow and a sense of loss. All these feelings are depressing and take a lot of your energy to maintain. You can minimize these depressing negative feelings if you change your focus from what you have lost to what your loved ones have gained. If they are elderly, then they are no longer in pain or limited by a failing physical body. They are now in a body made of higher frequency etheric energy that has no pain and allows them to function perfectly in the realm they are now in.

Death only changes the nature of the physical body, not mental, emotional or soul body. The person is not in the physical; it is in the three nonphysical bodies. They are the same person mentally, emotionally, spiritually and have the same personality they had before their physical body died. They have the ability to not only visit you, but also communicate with you if you are open for it. You may talk to them, ask for their help and guidance, ask them how they're doing, so you really have not lost them, you have only lost the physical body that your five senses related to.

They are not dead and gone they are simply with you in a different way. The passing away of their physical body does not change the love they have for you any more than it altered the love you have for them. What has changed is how you communicate with each other. Your deepest communication will mostly take place when you are in the alpha state and it will come through your subconscious mind when are asleep or in a meditative state. In almost all cases your loved ones are in a better body and situation than they were before they died. And do realize that they miss being with you physically even as you miss them.

Let's shift our focus and talk about the person who has died. Unless they have a very, very strong belief about what is going to happen to them after they leave their physical body, they will likely follow the experience of those who have had a near-death experience.

After hovering near the ceiling for a very brief time they will quickly travel to Heaven's entrance. They will find themselves at the entrance to the tunnel of light. They may be there alone, but more likely there will be loved ones and/or Angels with them supporting them and encouraging them to go into the tunnel of light, which is the entrance to what is called Heaven.

In my experience about 75% will choose to go into the tunnel and 25% will choose not to go into the tunnel but will remain in the astral plane. The Astral Plane is what they traveled through to get to the tunnel of light and where they are as they stand outside of the tunnel. We will now look at these two places and the types of life experiences they hold.

Heaven

For those that choose to go into the tunnel of light, the further they go in the tunnel, the higher the frequency. When they reach the frequency of their consciousness they are joined with their light body. Their light body is that part of them that did not come into physical embodiment with them, and in fact has never been in physical embodiment.

It contains all of the wisdom, knowledge and memories going back to when they were first given a soul. When their astral body and light body join and become one, there is a flash of light. In that flash of light all the memories of their recent physical lifetimes are downloaded into their light body and the two bodies merge, becoming one body with all the memories merged into their light body. As one being they will shoot upward and go into the heavenly realm. In essence, they have traded their physical body for their light body.

I have had the experience of standing outside of the tunnel of light and witnessing this in an out-of-body experience. It was the most emotional and meaningful experience I have ever had. Even as I write this, I am moved remembering the deepest emotions I have ever felt; the total unconditional love, the deepest peace I have ever known, the overwhelming feeling of being at one with the entire universe. The energy that affected me was coming from the tunnel. The feelings were so beautiful and strong I wanted to go into the tunnel, but I was stopped. An angel was standing in front of me holding up their hand with the palm facing me indicating, "STOP" and a firm voice saying, "It is not your time. You have work yet to do and there is Ortrun" (my wife). I was immediately back in my physical body. This is a memory I will never forget; the most meaningful experience I have ever had. I am so grateful I had it!

For most people when they enter the heavenly realm the first place they go is a room in the welcome center. Gathered there are all their loved ones from all past lives that are currently on the heavenly realm. There are so many hugs, so much love, so much joy - it is party time! It is a wonderful reunion! Old friendships are reestablished, memories are recalled, and there is so much love and joy it is absolutely beautiful to behold. As it gradually winds down there are usually two people that hold back and when they are alone they will say, "Come with us and we will take you home."

Where they take them will be the part of Heaven in which they will be most comfortable. It is that part of Heaven that is functioning at their level of consciousness. Jesus said, "In my father's house are many rooms." Each "room" is functioning in a narrow range of frequencies and is the same as the consciousness level of the people in that room.

In other words, everyone is very much like you! Even in Heaven you cannot escape living with you and now you are living with people very much like you! It is easier to see what you are like if you experience it with similar people. You will hopefully like and admire much that you see. However, there will likely be some things that will make you ask, "Oh my God, am I like that too!" It is then you start making a list of the changes you will want to make in your next physical lifetime.

You know that we all have free will and that we can never escape the consequences of the choices we have made. We are the creator of the person that we are now and the person we will become in the future. This is the power our free will gives us. The fact that we must live with our self now and in the hereafter is our reward/punishment. It is the law of cause and effect at work. God does not judge us! This makes us our own judge!

Heaven offers us the benefit of being surrounded by people very similar to our self because it is easier to see our self in others than to look within and self-analyze. We will find things in others that we really like, admire and respect and then realize we also have those same traits. In the same manner we will see things in others that we don't like and realize that we too have those same traits. This greatly facilitates self-evaluation and is most helpful in planning the growth they want to attain in their next physical incarnation.

Heaven isn't just about introspection and planning the next physical lifetime, it is also about being of service. There are many ways to be of service in the heavenly realm and there are also many ways that you can be of help to those that are still in physical form on Earth. In fact, the most popular job in Heaven is to be a guide to someone still in a physical body.

To qualify you first have to volunteer, second you have to be more advanced in consciousness then the physical person you are going to be over lighting. As a guide you will spend a lot of time overlighting them and helping them to stay on the life script that they prepared for themselves before they incarnated. Guides are restricted like everyone else by the law of noninterference.

Because Earth is a school designed to facilitate growth and raise consciousness, growth can be much faster than on the heavenly realm. When they catch up with you, you will leave and another more advanced guide will take your place. You may then choose to do that again for another person and wait to be selected or you may choose another vocation.

Keep in mind that the heavenly realm is very peaceful, there is no violence, there is a lot of support provided for each person; classes are available, individual teachers are available, as are counselors. But because there are few real challenges, growth is not as fast as it is here on the very challenging physical Earth. Heaven provides the opportunity for introspection, contemplation, planning and evaluation.

You do not have the distractions of providing for a physical body, raising a family, earning money, health challenges and staying physically safe. In other words, it is a great break from many responsibilities, giving you a time to relax and enjoy by giving the service you want to give and not having to do what is essential for survival. It is also a time to renew old relationships going back countless lifetimes, to express and experience love with them, to reminisce and to just enjoy each other's presence.

Because your body is not physical you have the opportunity to travel many different places in the universe, learning and satisfying your curiosity. On average a person will spend twice as much time on the heavenly realm as we spend on the physical realm. Thus, it can be said that *Heaven* is our *real home*, and Earth is where we go to school.

Astral Plane

Please use what you have just read as a contrast to what you are about to read as we deal with the 25% that chose not to go into the tunnel of light, the entrance to Heaven, but rather chose to stay in the *astral plane*. Why in the world would a person choose not to go into Heaven? In my experience there are three main reasons.

1. *Fear* keeps more people from going into Heaven than any other single cause. The fear says, "I'm not good enough. I'm going to be judged. I'm going to be punished. I could be going to hell."

2. *Attachment* is the second main reason people choose not to go into Heaven. The thing people are most apt to be attached to are *their* families who are still in physical bodies. They feel their families still need them, or they feel that they cannot go on without their family's support. Some other attachments are money, power and the need to control others. Some are attached to their

cars, and from time to time you hear of them being buried in their cars. Others might be attached to their house or items in their house, their jewelry or most anything else, including their social status.

3. *Addiction* includes not only addiction to drugs and alcohol, but there are many emotional addictions. Even when a person's physical body dies the desire for that drug is still in their mind, which does not die. If they feel they can't live without that drug they may choose not to go into the heavenly realm. Emotional addictions include such things as depression, illness, excitement, gambling, risk-taking, etc. Each of these emotional addictions has a payoff; depression and illness are rewarded with drugs and often recognition and attention. The emotional highs you feel when you win or succeed in business, sports, gambling, etc., can also be addictions. In addition to these three there are any number of reasons that a person may choose not to go into the heavenly realm. Some of them may even be positive, such as they want to stay back and help those that are in the astral plane.

What is this astral plane, where is it and why can't we see it? All good questions, let's explore some answers. Where is the astral plane? It is a plane that surrounds Earth extending up from Earth's surface to the bottom of the heavenly plane, which surrounds the astral plane. If it extends from Earth's surface upward, then why can't we see it?

We cannot see it because it is made of a different type of energy than our physical Earth energy. The astral plane is made of lower vibration of *etheric* energy. Heaven is made of higher vibration *etheric* energy thus making them both invisible to us. Our five senses are tuned to register only what is made of electro-magnetic energy. When the 25% of people who die get to the tunnel of light and choose not to enter Heaven but stay on the astral plane, the tunnel for them disappears.

So, what is the astral plane, what is it like? It is home to an unknown number of people that surely numbers in the hundreds of millions or even billions. They are human beings with an astral body. Their astral body is made up of their mental, emotional and soul bodies. Here on Earth we have a physical body that houses our astral body. On the heavenly plane they have an astral body plus a light body. The astral plane has a huge variety of people, in terms of levels of consciousness just as there are on Earth.

The lowest levels of the astral plane were referred to, by the Roman Catholic Church, as "Purgatory". The higher levels do not have names that I am aware of, but if you can imagine a city with its different levels of cultural, educational, intelligence, consciousness and wealth, it is the same on the astral plane. A new arrival will seek out a level in which they feel most comfortable, look for people they know or share interests with and can relate too.

They need to be cautious because the levels are all open and some power grabbing beings of lower consciousness will try using *fear* to control beings, taking some of their energy to use for their own purposes. The most powerful of these are called Dark Lords. There are others on the astral planes who try to attach themselves to people's physical, mental or emotional bodies here on Earth, so we need to learn how to protect ourselves here too.

The increasing frequencies brought about by the ascension of Earth and its life forms are impacting both the heavenly realm and the astral plane. This was made clear to me about five years ago. When I sat down one morning to do the morning clearing of astral plane beings who now wanted to go to Heaven and had come for help. I could see/sense them hovering outside the house and when they went into the tunnel of light I could see them, and my physical body jerked. Up to that point there was only one tunnel of light. Suddenly there were two tunnels.

Let me pause for a moment and explain what a clearing is and what the tunnel of light is. For over 35 years people who have died, both recently and hundreds of years ago, come to me to be helped when they are ready to leave the astral plane and move into the heavenly plane. When they died and chose not to go into the tunnel of light, the tunnel disappeared, and they now need help to find it.

Several psychics have told me I have a flashing neon sign on the astral plane that says, "Come to me I can help." And that is the help I give them. Doing this work, I believe is a part of what I planned for this lifetime. I began by asking my spirit family to protect my wife Ortrun, myself, and our house, by placing us in a beautiful protective bubble of light and love.

The ones who want to be moved on are already at our house waiting for me when I wake up each morning. I ask that the astral plane souls' dearest, closest loved ones come from the heavenly realm and be with them. I then ask the heavenly loved ones to lead the astral plane souls to the Angels of Transition who can lead them to the tunnel of light. I also ask the loved ones to stay with them to support and encourage them to go into the tunnel. The astral plane souls almost always choose to enter the tunnel.

This went on for about 30 years until one morning when I went into the meditative state to do the morning clearing and instead of one tunnel of light there were two tunnels of light. I did my usual clearing, and all went well. Because I am a person who has a need to understand, the next morning before doing the clearing I went into meditative state and asked, "Why is there a second tunnel?"

The beings in the spirit realm that work with me stated, "The lower part of the astral plane has been moved to another third-dimensional Earth-like planet that is not slated for ascension at this time. Those on the astral plane will only see one tunnel, the one that is appropriate for them based on their level of consciousness." There have been two tunnels ever since then.

People, when they die that are on the ascension path and going to ascend with our ascending Earth, are going through the original tunnel of light. Those that are not yet ready to ascend are being given more time to grow in consciousness while on this other third-dimensional Earth-like planet. The only exception that I'm aware of, is some extraordinary light workers who have volunteered to incarnate on this lower third-dimensional planet, so they can help teach and be spiritual leaders. Such beautiful beings these light workers must be.

In the last several years more of the lower portions of the astral plane and Heaven have been moved to this other third-dimensional planet. Also, both Heaven and the astral plane of our ascending planet can now accommodate people with higher levels of consciousness. This means not only is Earth ascending but that the astral plane and Heaven are also ascending.

Those on the astral plane, as well as in the heavenly plane, can see and hear what they choose to focus on here on the Earth plane. Without a physical body they are very limited in what they can do on the Earth plane, but they can be aware of their loved ones.

They can send them thoughts, visit them in their dreams and in life threatening events give warnings and even in rare cases take physical action. In other words, in a limited manner, relationships may be continued; death does not break the bonds of love. As noted earlier the second major cause for not going into the heavenly realm is the love of family.

The important thing to note is that going into Heaven allows you not only to continue your relationship with your physical family but because you now have the much greater wisdom coming from your light body you can be more helpful to them than if you had stayed on the astral plane. Because Heaven is a much more pleasant place to be and affords far more opportunities for growth, learning, and service than the astral plane, it is always the better choice. Also, when you decide that you want to come back for another physical lifetime this can only be done from the heavenly plane.

On every level of the astral plane most people come together creating groups of like-minded people. These groups may become like an extended family. Most of the groups have a leader and they are referred to as Lords. One of the functions of the Lords is to keep the people in their group safe. People may stay on the astral plane for a short period of time or a very long period of time. At some point most will change their mind and regret not having gone into the tunnel of light. That is when they begin to seek help in finding the tunnel of light. This is where I, and others that are called spiritual doulas, fit into the larger picture.

I do not understand why someone in physical human form needs to be involved in helping people move from the astral plane to the heavenly plane, but it appears to be necessary. When I started this work 35 years ago I would do it daily and there might be a half a dozen or so that were ready to be moved.

Now it is in the hundreds and even the thousands that are waiting each morning and each evening to move out of the astral plane and into the heavenly realm. The increasing frequencies not only affect Earth but also the astral plane and apparently making it more and more uncomfortable for those that are there.

It is apparent that the increasing frequencies that are affecting Earth and people, called "Ascension symptoms", are also affecting the astral plane. Because Earth is a teaching planet, where change is virtually constant, though we are experiencing discomfort, we are better able to adjust than those on the lower levels of astral plane. They are more uncomfortable than we are, and thus more are seeking to escape their discomfort. This explains the large number of astral plane souls that are now choosing to leave and go into the heavenly realm.

Because there are people at different levels of consciousness on the astral plane there are dark Lords who try to recruit as many people to follow them as possible. They then take much of each person's power, strengthening their control over the entire group. There are many groups of Dark Lords that work to create fear upon people on Earth so that they can use the fear to enhance their power. Fear is the primary tool used by the Dark Lords and they are the most potent force in purgatory and the levels immediately above purgatory. They are always probing the higher levels of the astral plane for additional followers.

They also reach down into the Earth plane trying to gain control over the physical bodies and minds of individuals, especially individuals who are in positions of power. I am happy to report that in my experience most of the Dark Lords are now gone. They have been given the choice of either going to The Light School or being removed to the third-dimensional Earth-like planet where they would take on a life form determined by their level of consciousness. It could be as low as a spider or a snake.

Ninety-eight to ninety-nine percent choose the Light School which will bring them to a much higher level of consciousness and allow them to remain with our soon to be fifth-dimensional planet. The lower-level archangels have taken on the responsibility of overseeing rounding up the Dark Lords and giving them this choice.

Some of the souls that chose not to go into the heavenly realm because of addictions, especially the chemical addictions, are becoming more and more desperate. The only way they can satisfy their craving is if they can attach themselves to a person with a physical body.

The only way they can attach them to itself to a physical person is if there is a crack or an opening in that person's aura. The aura is a field of energy that radiates from our physical body and creates a field of protective energy around us. The auric field can develop a crack or a hole due to things like being deeply depressed, being very negative, having had too much to drink or having taken strong drugs, even prescription drugs.

This allows astral plane entities who may have been watching us, waiting for our aura to fracture, to slip inside our auric field and to influence us by amplifying the behavior that is going to allow them to satisfy their chemical or emotional addiction. They cannot achieve the high without a physical body, so they have to find someone else that does. This is part of the reason for the great increase in drug addiction.

In closing this section, a word of advice. When the time approaches for you to leave your physical body ask some of your loved ones who you feel are in Heaven to come and be with you, guide you and advise you. Also, ask the Angels to be with you and to lead you to the tunnel of light. When you get to the tunnel of light do not hesitate, *go in*! There is no judgment, there is no punishment. These man-made beliefs are *false*. There is *nothing to fear*! There is *love, growth, service, joy and peace* and when ready for your next physical lifetime, it can only happen if you are in Heaven. In contrast, the astral plane offers no future, little if any personal growth, no hope, no light body and for many a lot of despair.

CHAPTER 10

INNER EARTH

I n the year 2000, John Davis and Denise Iwaniw Francisco were leading a trip to Mount Shasta in northern California. Every time I read the email announcing the trip, I heard in a voice in my head say, "If you go you will meet an Inner Earth person." I very much wanted to go but the money was not available, so we did not sign up. Mount Shasta is known to be a portal to Inner Earth. My spirit family had other plans. The physical family situation changed, and it became necessary for us to go out to Oregon, which is not far from Mount Shasta.

We were able to arrange our schedules so that we joined the Mount Shasta group at the foot of the mountain on the day they were going up. About halfway up Mount Shasta is an area known as Panther Meadows. This is a relatively flat area and many known events involving space beings and Inner Earth people have occurred here.

Denise Iwaniw Francisco, who was leading the first event, told us to find a place that felt sacred to us and to meditate there; and to allow to happen whatever is going to happen. I chose a spot next to a little six-inch stream of the snowmelt coming off the glacier at the top of the mountain. I quickly dropped into a deep meditation.

Across the stream from me, close enough that I could reach out and touch her; a woman began to emerge from Earth. She did not come all the way out but far enough that we were at the same eye level. Her skin was indigo. Her robe and conical shaped hat were also indigo. The whites of her eyes really stood out. She said, "I understand you want to learn about Inner Earth." I said, "Yes, what can you tell me." She said,

> Your scientists do not understand the nature of Earth. Earth has two crusts that average about 400 miles each in thickness and rotate in opposite directions. They function together exactly like your electric motors. The friction between the two creates the lava and keeps it hot and semi liquid, and it in turn acts as a lubricant. In the very center of Earth there is a small red white sun. We revolve around the sun and do not have night as you do. It is light all the time.

> The temperature and climate throughout Inner Earth is moderate. Because of the moderate temperature and 24-hour Sun our vegetation thrives. Plants grow faster than they do on the surface of Earth and our vegetation is very lush and beautiful, flowers abound. Our topography is very similar to yours; we have mountains and oceans, there are planes, forests, meadows, rivers, lakes and streams.

> We do have many wild animals, more abundant then on Earth's surface. We do not hunt them but rather enjoy them. Because we are not a threat to them and because food is so abundant for them they often become almost like pets. This allows us to live in peace and harmony with them and if one gets injured or sick they will often come to us for help.

> We came here from the continent of Lemuria. We are a very peaceful people even to the point that we will not defend ourselves if attacked. The Atlanteans were threatening to attack us and we wanted to avoid any physical violence. A few of us were already at a sixth-

dimensional level of consciousness and were able to create portals into Inner Earth and take with us all of our people.

Many of our animals and some peace loving Atlanteans, who lived among us also came with us. We then closed the portals that we had created. Without portals the Atlanteans could not follow us, as their consciousness was not high enough to go through the solid crusts of Earth. We then began rebuilding our Lemurian society and culture here in Inner Earth.

Of the people in Inner Earth 65% are now sixth dimensional, 25% are fifth dimensional and 10% are high fourth-dimensional. In Inner Earth, we stress spiritual growth and almost all our population is growing in consciousness. Together we have created a society and a living style that many of you would likely refer to as "Heaven on Earth".

We see you who live on Earth's surface as a part of our family. After all we are all humans living on the same planet. We are looking forward to the day that we can be with you and that you can come and visit us. What is keeping that from happening is we very much value peace and we abhor violence. When you become more peaceful it will please us greatly to spend time together. To us you are like cousins that we have been separated from and we are anxious to be reunited with you. We see your consciousness increasing and that pleases us. When it is safe we will join you on the surface and, if you choose help you build a fifth-dimensional culture, society and religion.

She then began to sink into Earth and was quickly out of sight. In her presence I felt peace and a great sense of sincerity. She did not give me her name and I regret not having asked for it. As she was describing Inner Earth it was as if I was there in person not only seeing it but also experiencing it. Little did I know that encounter was but an introduction to what would follow.

A year or so after our return from Mt. Shasta, another Inner Earth person began to visit me in my meditation. Her name is Aleah. Her job, as I understand it, is to help prepare us surface dwellers to meet with and be comfortable with our Inner Earth cousins. Aleah takes individuals and groups of people, who are in an "out of body state", to Inner Earth where they can experience it first-hand.

In my first trip to Inner Earth she and I were alone. She gave me a wonderful tour and it was exactly as it had been described to me at Mount Shasta. The next two times I was with not only Aleah, but also a group of people. I believe I was along to help these other people be comfortable and not be afraid.

All three times, at the end of the tour, she led us into a building in which there were a number of - I'm not sure what to call them because I've not experienced anything like it before - I'm going to call them consciousness-raising chambers. These were round chambers with a flat padded comfortable surface that was about waist high. You lay down on your back and a transparent canopy was lowered over you. Within a minute or so you were completely relaxed, and it was only natural to close your eyes.

With eyes closed the clear canopy became colored in a kaleidoscope of beautiful pastel shades. Each color, it felt like, was emitting energy at the frequency of its color. I could see the color with my closed eyes, but I could also feel the energy inside my body, in every organ and every cell. I could also sense the energy in my head, more specifically in my brain.

There was an aroma in the chamber and it kept changing as the color changed. There was also sound almost like music. It too changed with the color and aroma. Something was happening, I don't know what, but it felt good, as if my mental, physical and emotional bodies were being tuned.

When it was done I felt great and I asked Aleah what this machine did. She said, "It balances your physical, mental and emotional bodies and raises their frequency one or two frequencies higher than when the treatment began. You might view it as a consciousness-raising device.

It was a very pleasant experience and I believe its purpose was to prepare us, for what I am not quite sure, but I do believe it has something to do with preparing us for coming relations with our Inner Earth cousins by making us more like them. There was no sense of time, so I do not know how long I was in the chamber. When the procedure was over, the glass canopy opened and although in many ways I was the same but, in many ways, I felt I had changed. I do not remember exactly what happened after stepping out of the consciousness-raising chamber, I only knew I was back in my physical body.

This is the totality of my experience with Inner Earth and their people, but I do know that they are to be playing an important role in the ascension of Earth and all life upon it in the years to come. Their high level of consciousness has raised the frequency of the inner crust of Earth, which has helped the outer crust raise its frequency faster and with less disruption, such as earthquakes, volcanic eruptions, etc.

When it is safe for them to come to the surface they will become our teachers, way showers and healers, showing us what it is we can be as we continue to raise our consciousness eventually to their level. Presently they are holding the frequency of Earth higher than it would be otherwise. Because of them, and the work of the light workers and other spirit beings working with us, the frequency of Earth has and continues to increase. Meanwhile the collective consciousness of humanity has also moved up.

Another role that our Inner Earth family may be playing in the near future is they may be providing a safe place for millions of us if it is determined that the passage of Nibiru it poses too much danger for those living on Earth's surface. Inner Earth will be affected by Nibiru's closeness to Earth but not nearly to the extent that the surface of Earth will be. They will not experience the possible flooding, intense earthquakes, and dust laden in atmosphere. I am told that during our stay in Inner Earth we will be able to use the consciousness-raising device we have talked about. I am sure these will be most popular among virtually all of us.

In the last several years there has been a noticeable increase in the number of people coming to me for Life Script Readings who are from Inner Earth. I am under the impression that more individuals from Inner Earth are one by one coming to the surface to help us, to teach us, to help us raise our collective consciousness. I also feel they want to experience and be part of our Ascension and the Ascension of the planet. And perhaps also to help many of us who may be going to Inner Earth to feel more comfortable there and adjust more quickly.

I do know they are beautiful people, wise, loving, concerned and caring. I'm looking forward to spending more time with them in the future and am hoping to grow to be more like them.

CHAPTER 11

OUR LIFE SCRIPT

One of the purposes of our spirit family is to help keep us on our "life script" so we can achieve the goals we had set for ourselves. Before a person can come into physical embodiment on this planet they have to have a plan that says what personal growth they are going to achieve and what service they are going to give. With a planned destination it allows progress to be measured.

Many consider Earth to be a school that we come to learn certain lessons. As you can see our life is very important and for most people it usually takes them 20 to 25 years to prepare. Keeping us on script is one of the most import services our spirit family does for us. Because of the law of non-interference that governs what the spirit realm can and cannot do, our spirit family cannot directly intervene in our life.

Our spirit family can influence situations that will give us the opportunity to learn what we said we wanted to learn or to give the service we said we wanted to give. They may influence us through our dreams, or with thoughts that pop into our mind. If we choose to follow them they may guide us so that we meet people or have challenges that give us the opportunity to fulfill a part of our script.

When we were still on the heavenly plane writing our life script we were not doing this alone. The angels, who are now a major portion of our spirit family, were working with us along with the higher aspects of our self. If we needed additional help all we needed to do was ask and help was gladly given.

There is far more planning for our lifetime than just the life script. We had to choose our parents, siblings, major and minor challenges, opportunities, spouse or spouses, children, and vocation, especially if it was going to play a major role in our life. We also planned our closest friends, significant events, and all major and most minor experiences.

Nothing happens in our life that has significance that we did not plan as long as we remain on script. We even plan many of the minor events and casual relationships. It is all there for a purpose that was planned by you. A strong suggestion: when an event occurs in your life, take a few moments and ask yourself the question "what am I to learn from this?" To get the answer you need to listen and be open to hear. It is best if this can be done in the alpha (meditative) state.

As you grow in your consciousness and are in a meditative state you may talk with your spirit family and ask them questions. Because they view you and your life situation not only from a higher level of consciousness, but also from a broader perspective they can see options and possibilities that you may not be aware of. When you do this please be discerning.

If the information you receive is positive and empowering it is likely coming from your spirit family. If the information you are being given is negative, hurtful to others, or boosts your own ego, it could well be coming from a low source such as your ego. To prevent this when we are asking questions or asking for guidance, we always add, "That it be for my highest good and the highest good of all involved." Working as one with your spirit family in this way can make available to you much of the information that is available from some of the higher dimensions.

You may also ask your spirit family to assist you in performing tasks or solving a problem that are a part of your life script. These can be situations outside of you, such as overcoming problems in a relationship or finding a job. Or you can ask them for help and guidance in learning to be more loving, forgiving, sensitive, patient, giving, etc.

They are glad when you ask as it gives satisfaction and even pleasure knowing they have helped. Their greatest joy comes from assisting you to grow in consciousness. This raises the frequency in all four of your bodies, physical, mental, emotional and spiritual. The changes made to your three nonphysical bodies can have a long lasting, even eternal effect. In my experience almost all light workers life script include growth in consciousness, balance between head and heart, opening their high heart, and connecting with and becoming one with their spirit family.

In order to attain this growth, it is normal to ask your spirit family for help in keeping your chakras functioning at the highest possible frequency. This will fill all of your four bodies, physical, mental, emotional, and spirit body with high-frequency positive energy. It will not only strengthen and empower these bodies but it also means that you will be radiating beautiful energy through your aura and everywhere you go your aura's energy will be impacting everyone you physically get close to. If in your life script you stated that you were going to do healing work and your physical body needs healing, or someone else needs healing, ask your spirit family for their help. Together you will have so much more energy to affect healing than if you are using only your own energy.

These are but two examples of how you can work with your spirit family and how they can help you give what you planned to give and attain the growth wanted. By joining forces with your spirit family your combined energy is much more than just the sum total as it increases exponentially. This makes it easier and quicker to accomplish both personal growth and the service you want to give.

Your spirit family, except in emergencies, is limited in the energy they can project into this physical reality. Not being physical themselves, they need a physical person. Being one with you allows them to ground their energy through your physical body. They can most effectively affect the physical world through your physical body, so asking for their help creates a win-win situation. Instead of hesitating to ask for help look for opportunities where they can help and then ask. To repeat, this will make staying on and fulfilling your life script easier and may even allow you to go beyond what you had planned.

As you can see your life script and your spirit family are interrelated. To fulfill your life script without the help and guidance of your spirit family would be extremely difficult. You do not necessarily have to be consciously aware of them, though it is helpful if you are, but you need to be open to at least their subtle guidance. Their help is invaluable, but it is not a one-way street.

You see, though you are not aware of it, every day you are doing so much for them. You may ask, what in the world can I do for them and not know that I'm doing it? The answer is, you are their teacher. You, with your physical body, are the means through which they can give and help you, others in your life and the planet. Their help is greatly needed and deeply appreciated during this time of ascension. You are each facilitating each other to be and do what you are here to do.

I hope you can sense the importance of having a spirit family and the value in not only acknowledging their presence but also beginning to communicate and work with them. It is hard to imagine anything that you cannot accomplish with the entire spirit family and you working as one with the combined multidimensional knowledge.

I hope you can understand why becoming one with your higher self is so important and the major role it plays in your ascension process.

CHAPTER 12

OUR SPIRIT FAMILY

I n our world it is impossible to be alone. In my experience, we have spirits beings over lighting us from birth. Many of these same spirit beings have been with us throughout our entire life and in fact, have been with us through many of our past lives. They know us better than we know our self. Most of our spirit family is with us 24/7; the rest are on call.

The fact that they cannot be detected by our five senses is most likely the reason that most are unaware of their presence. But their presence cannot be kept secret that much longer, because an increasing number of the children being born, with what is referred to as Crystal energy, can feel, see and hear them.

If 70% or more of their energy field is of the Crystal nature, their spirit family will be as real to them as their physical family. These special children can see, hear, and feel things that are beyond the normal range of the five senses of most people.

Our spirit was helping us on the heavenly realm before we were even conceived. They played a major role in helping us plan this lifetime. It took most of more than 20 years to complete our life plan and our spirit family was helping along the way.

The spirit families are different for normal people (those who evolved on Earth through evolution) and those who came from elsewhere. The spirit family of normal people is made up of between six and twenty-one angels (the higher their consciousness, the more angels) and one to two guides from Heaven giving them a total of between seven and twenty-three. In the chapter on "What it means to be a human" we covered those people who did not evolve here but came from the angelic realm, higher dimensions of space, the spirit realm and elsewhere, so I am not to bore you by repeating it.

Just know they all have advanced DNA and have varying amounts of Indigo and Crystal energy. They all volunteered to lower their frequency (consciousness) so they could came here to assist with the ascension of Earth and humanity. All of these people, when they awaken, will be light workers. Their spirit families are made up of 21-22 angels (only those from the angelic realm have 22), one to two heavenly guides, two to four higher aspects of themselves, one to two master teachers and one ascended master teacher (their consciousness has to be high enough to attract the teachers). So, this means they have 24-31 in their spirit family.

Our spirit family is with us for the following reasons:

1. To keep us on our life script.

2. To help us when we ask (they are the ones that answer our prayers).

3. To learn from us. The angels and higher aspects of our self have never been in physical bodies or in a dimension this low and never experienced anything that our physical, mental, emotional and spiritual bodies experience. And they are curious.

4. They love us. Our angels have been with us through many life times and the higher aspects of our self have been with us in all of our human life times.

Let's look at these four reasons in more detail.

1) When we were born we left our memory in Heaven in our light body and we will be reunited with it when we return to Heaven. Without our memory, if we came without a plan we would flounder like a ship without a rudder. We leave our memory behind so we can start with a clean slate and not be held back by guilt or energy from our past lives. Our life script is our rudder giving us control and a destination to steer for. It gives meaning and direction to our life. This is why it is important to be aware of and communicate with our spirit family, trust them and follow the guidance they are giving us.

2) Do you know anyone whose life has always gone smooth with no big bumps in the road? I have not, and I am going to guess that you haven't either. One of the main teaching tools on the planet is overcoming problems and meeting challenges. When these come into your life have ever prayed asking for help? Did you receive help? I believe help is always given, but not always received, because we were not listening. It is our spirit that always answers, but because prayer is a monologue and when we say "Amen", our mental focus is immediately back in the physical world, so we often miss what our spirit family told us. I rarely pray when I want help; I meditate. In the meditative state you can dialog with your spirit family getting not only the answer you want but also clarification if needed, and you are not going to miss the answer. Our spirit family wants you to ask help. It gives them satisfaction to be able to help and to see you move ahead so to ask and receive is a win-win situation.

3) It is hard to believe that we teach our angels and the higher aspects of our self, but we do. As far as I know most all learning in the universe, on all dimensions, comes out of experience. Beings on higher dimensions can observe the lower dimensions and learn a lot, but to fully understand it and

the beings in those dimensions it has to be personally experienced. Curiosity is a common trait throughout the universe and this is why higher-dimensional beings want to understand us and our world. One of the ways they do this without coming here totally in all of their fullness is they send a surrogate, that is an aspect or a part of their consciousness who has a body made out of the material frequency and in the form of that place. This is what most of the light workers are, but they volunteered to come because their higher self wanted not only to experience this dimension, but also to assist it with its ascension. Curiosity satisfied, and service given—a win-win experience.

4) The angels have spent so much time with you over numerous lifetimes; they have developed such a love for you that they keep coming back so they can be with you. You have become like an extension of them creating union, a oneness. To your higher selves you are a lower-dimensional part of them, almost like their child. Their bond with you is an unbreakable love. In meditation ask to feel their presence and talk with them. I think it may feel like going to your childhood home. If so, know that someday you will go home, and what a celebration there will be.

You now know that you are never alone and always are surrounded by loving, wise, powerful beings who want you to ask for their help when you feel you need it. They cannot help if do not ask, but can only watch you worry, fret and be stressed out, and wonder why you are not asking. It is better to love yourself and not cause your loving spirit family concern. Their dream for you and themselves is for you to become *one* with them, one will, one consciousness and one energy. If you do this life will flow much more smoothly and the challenges, instead of being mountains, will seem like foothills.

CHAPTER 13
ANGELS

*A*rchangels—to me these are the most fascinating and powerful beings in our universe. The four highest archangels are made from the energy and carry a consciousness just below Christ Michael, the creator of our universe. The first thing Christ Michael created in the universe according to *The Urantia Book* was Archangel Gabriel. Gabriel holds the highest energy and consciousness in the universe and is second in command of the universe.

Gabriel is the chief Archangel in charge of the entire angelic realm including archangels through the Devas. Christ Michael then created three other archangels to assist Gabriel. Their names are, *Raphael, Uriel* and *Michael.* Each of these archangels is responsible for a portion of the angelic realm. They each have a huge amount of Christ Michael's energy and consciousness within themselves.

From that energy and consciousness Raphael, Uriel and Michael have each created a family of archangels to assist them. Each of these archangels have a little lower energy frequency than the archangel they came from. This process was repeated creating many different levels of archangels. The lowest levels of archangels are the ones that began creating angels and each is the head of their angelic family.

All archangels are unique, just as we are each different, so each angelic family is unique and each in that family of angel is different. Each angelic family has its areas of expertise and this explains why angels do not all look the same. Their size and shape fit the work they do.

Over time, as the universe has expanded, and more archangels are needed, instead of being created by an archangel, angels in that archangel's family can be promoted to the position of archangel. Just as the number of archangels can grow, so can the number of angels. When a Deva has learned all, it can in the Devic realm; it may be asked by an archangel who needs more angels to join its angelic family. In this way an angelic family can grow as Devas become angels.

Each Archangel has a large field of divine conscious energy that is coming from Christ Michael, and this is not only life force energy but also is the *soul* of that archangel. Out of this *soul* energy each Archangel creates its own angelic family thus bringing the entire angelic realm into being. Because each angel then carries some of the personality traits and the soul energy and consciousness of its creator, each Archangel angelic family is unique and harmonious. This gives each angelic family its own distinctive personality. This allows each family with its different interests and abilities to fill a niche in the universe in which it can best function and serve allowing all of the needs of the universe to be met.

We tend to think that all Angels look the same but that is not true. Some Angels have wings because they are needed in the work they do. Some Angels have the ability to change their appearance so that those humans who can see them will be comfortable in their presence. You see we humans aren't the only species that Angels deal with. Like us, Angels have different personalities, appearances and abilities. They are as individual as we are, however there are some common traits that most of them have.

They have a great deal of love and they welcome the opportunity to share their love to all who are open to receive it. They tend to be joyful, at times even exuberant. They have compassion, are caring and always desiring to be of service. They are non-judgmental, accepting and understanding. Their energy and consciousness are at least as high as or higher than the most evolved human beings on the planet.

They do not work in the timeline of past, present, and future. They work in the timeline of *now*; thus, they are very patient. We are one of the sources of their joy. When we ask for their help, and especially when we are open to receive their help, they are exceedingly joyful. Which means, we should never hesitate to ask because when we do we create a win-win situation; we both benefit.

Because of the law of noninterference, it is mandatory that you *ask* for the help you want. All of us have angels over lighting us 24/7. In my experience, each light worker has 21 – 22 Angels and they have been with you for many lifetimes. They know you better than you know yourself. They have so much love for you they choose to stay with you through many lifetimes, including this lifetime.

In fact, they even helped you plan this lifetime. They also choose you because you are their teacher, and the fact that they keep choosing you again and again indicates that you must be a good teacher. I am also sure another factor in choosing to be with you again is the tremendous love they have for you. They over light you, know what you think and how you feel, plus they see what you do, and all of this allows them to better understand the physical, mental emotional and spiritual nature of humans who are in physical form.

Angels are curious, especially about us. They have never directly experienced physical matter, a physical body, giving birth, raising children, physical pain, eating food, loss and death. Our Angels chose us because they're interested in the lessons that we are learning. They have become emotionally attached to us and they want to protect and guide us. Because in their realm time does not exist and since they can see the past, present and potential future they can be aware of far more options and probabilities then we can be aware of. They cannot know our absolute future because we have free will.

So, it behooves us to ask for their guidance and help so we can make the best decisions that are for our highest good and the highest good of all who these decisions and actions are going to impact.

Angels do have some restrictions; they are not allowed to interfere with anyone's personal experience. They recognize that each of those experiences is for your benefit; they are *our* lessons. However sometimes a lesson or challenge can be overwhelming, and help is needed. Your Angels are able to help you *only if you ask*. This is a mandatory requirement for getting help from your Angels.

By asking they are not interfering; you are still the one in control of what and how you learn. The Angels are only assisting you in the learning process, not removing or solving the problem for you.

Your Angels have a dream that involves you and them. They would like to be among your very best friends. They would like you to be aware of their presence, of their loving you and wanting the very best for you. They would like you to communicate with them, asking them for help an

d inviting them to share much of your life with them. To them, together you are a family, and working together you can accomplish so much more than if you are trying to do it alone. By living as a family, you are living in the field of energy created by your Angels. Their energy is joyful, loving, peaceful and wise. What you are contributing to the family is you have a physical body, which the angels do not. If they want to impact anything in this physical world it must be done through you. Together you can do things that cannot be accomplished separately. Again, a win-win situation.

The most effective way to communicate with your angelic family is in the meditative state where you're working simultaneously out of your conscious and subconscious minds. It is the subconscious mind that connects most completely with them and can hear or sense their presence and their desires or advice. Because your conscious mind is awake and active it also hears and feels what is being said and done.

The goal is to live in the world in such a way that you have one foot in the physical world, and the other foot in the spirit world, the world of your Angels. This will keep your consciousness at a high level and allow you, wherever you are and whatever you are doing, to ground the energy and the consciousness of your angels. This also allows them to share their wisdom and use their angelic energy. This is not only going to improve the quality of your life, but the quality of all the people you are close to. Give it a try; you might like it.

The Fallen Angels

Are all Angels good or is there such a thing as bad Angels? The answer to that depends on your perspective. From one perspective it would say not all are good because some are fallen Angels. From the perspective of the highest archangels they might say, "Yes, all are good." Why the difference? Because the highest archangels have asked two other archangels to do what they felt was necessary to save all life on planet Earth.

From my perspective, much of what the fallen angels appear to do is wrong. Their names you are familiar with, they are *Satan* and *Lucifer*. The common belief is that they are "bad guys" because of having done many evil deeds. If this is true how can the archangels consider all angels to be good?

To repeat what is in another part of this book, the universe has a problem. Seventy-five percent of inhabited planets making the transition from third and fourth-dimensional levels of consciousness into the fifth dimension ended up destroying life on their planet. Technology advanced much faster than spirituality and consciousness.

When leaders of lower consciousness were more interested in service to self than service to others and valued wealth and power more than life, the technology often was misused. If this resulted in war using nuclear weapons, or polluting the atmosphere, water or soil the planet could become uninhabitable.

The plan for the ascension of Earth to correct this problem was to have a volunteer planet, which is Earth, experience the same conditions that led to all life being destroyed on those other planets. This meant that those conditions were to be created here on Earth. That meant lowering the consciousness of the people on Earth and developing technology at a faster rate than spirituality, thus creating the same imbalance that is the root cause of life being destroyed on a planet.

Those conditions have now been created on Earth as most of us are aware and we are now in the beginning process of solving all these issues. These solutions, once proven to work here on planet Earth, will then be taken to other planets going through the same transition from the third dimension to the fifth dimension. In the long run this will save countless lives and prolong the productive lives of many planets.

Archangel Satan volunteered to keep the consciousness low on the astral plane. The second Archangel, Lucifer, volunteered to do the same on the surface of the planet. So, it can be seen that what they were doing in the short run was detrimental to humanity, but in the long run would save humanity and the life-sustaining ability of Earth and many other planets.

Yes, they can be called angels of darkness but the darkness was only temporary. When Satan's works is done, his outer satanic covering will be removed, and he will resume being the beautiful Archangel that he truly is. Lucifer's job on the planet is progressing nicely but is not yet completed. It should be completed in the next two to five years. When done, he too will resume being his true angelic self. Meanwhile part two of the plan is beginning to be implemented. This part is called the *ascension*.

We owe lots of loving gratitude to these two brave Archangels who were willing to lower themselves into the deepest depths of darkness and Hell in order that we here on planet Earth might be saved, so *thank you Satan and Lucifer* for a job well done!

CHAPTER 14
DEVAS

The spirit realm is a vast arena with many different types of beings, each with their own functions. In this chapter we are going to focus on the beings that have the greatest impact on human life on our planet. They are the Devas. Devas, also known as nature spirits, I see as pre-angels. By that I mean when a Deva has learned all it can as a Deva it may enter into the lowest level of the angelic realm.

Devas are the soul aspect of all that is made out of electromagnetic energy, that is, all that we are aware of through our five senses. Devas are the spirit foundation, a tiny aspect of the creator's consciousness of everything made out of electromagnetic energy. There are a vast variety of Devas as we will see. Without the Devas Earth and all in, on and above it would not exist.

They are the creator's presence in everything that is made out of electromagnetic energy. They are, in essence, the creator expressing through a group soul. Both the group soul and each individual Deva have consciousness, free will, curiosity and Earth energy. Devas, so far as I know, are only in the first through fifth dimensions. Let's look more closely at what Devas look like and the role they play on our world.

What are they and what do they do? People who are known as sensitives—and they usually have Crystal energy—have greater than normal sensitivity and can often sense what many of us cannot see, smell or taste. Some of these people can see Devas and describe them verbally and in pictures as being "fairies" or "nature spirits". Devas are on an evolutionary path. As they gain experience and knowledge they will work with more evolved life forms. The Devas begin working with lower frequencies of energy, like the materials that make up Earth's crust. They are not the rock and minerals themselves but are the conscious energy of the creator holding the frequency that manifests as the rock and minerals.

When they have mastered all that can be learned at that level of consciousness they will move to substances that are at higher frequencies. In this way all frequencies that make up our Earth, its environment and life forms, have the spirit foundation for their physical existence. This allows the creator of our universe to not only know what is going on throughout the universe at all times but also to gain an in-depth understanding of everything in the universe.

The more evolved Devas work with more evolved life forms, such as the organs in human physical bodies and the more evolved animals. The less evolved Devas work with lower life forms such as bacteria, viruses, mold and fungus. The Devas are the spiritual foundation of everything, at least in our world. The Devas bring the life energy and the Creators consciousness to everything that has life.

Everything that we can sense through our five senses has its Devas. Two types of Devas that we are in close contact with are the air Devas and the water Devas. These two substances are vital to sustain human, animal, and plant life. They work closely together as it is the air that carries the moisture in the form of humidity and clouds that bring rain.

I would like to share a personal story with you that verifies the existence of Devas and shows the power they have. In the fall of 2017 one of the most powerful hurricanes ever recorded, named Irma, was approaching Florida.

All the weather forecasters' models were saying it was going to go up the entire peninsula of Florida with hurricane force winds. It was a force five hurricane with winds recording as high as 185 mph – 200 miles in diameter. When it was one hour away from making landfall at Naples, Florida, I went into meditation.

I was asking that our daughter and son-in-law's condo in Tarpon Springs, Florida where we spend four months each winter and the surrounding area, be protected. While I was in the meditative state, my spirit family said, "You are asking for the wrong thing." I then asked what I should be asking for, and they said, "Focus on the hurricane."

I did that and at once found myself in an out-of-body experience. I was looking down and could see the entire hurricane with 200 miles of swirling grey clouds. There were 200 – 400 dark lords dancing and having a party on top of the clouds. They live on fear and this massive powerful hurricane was creating so much fear in people, which gave them tremendous amounts of energy, so it was party time. They also fed some of the energy back into the storm to keep it strong.

Thank God I have dealt with dark lords before, so I knew what to do. I asked archangels to come and deal with the dark lords and they whisked them away. I was then floating beneath the clouds in 185 mile an hour winds, with the clouds above and the gulf below. Thank God I was not in physical form because the winds were horrendous.

The air Devas were having a ball, they were so excited! It was as if they were on a roller coaster at Disney World. Communicating with the Devas, mind to mind, I said, "You are really enjoying this, aren't you?" They had big grins on their face, laughing, dancing and so excited. They nodded their yes!

I then said, again mind to mind, "I know you have a job to do, to help cleanse Earth but at the rate that you are doing it you are going to knock down trees, kill people and destroy their property."

The Devas had gotten so caught up in their fun and excitement they forgot about what they were doing. They hung their heads and I felt the shame they felt for acting in this irresponsible way. There were of course, millions of people, not only in Florida, but also throughout the country praying that the people and property be protected from Irma.

One hour later when the hurricane landed at Naples, Florida it was a Category 4 hurricane and it continued to weaken as it traveled up the Florida peninsula. By the time it got halfway up the peninsula of Florida to Tampa and St. Petersburg it was a tropical storm.

What I learned from this is:

1. The air Devas control how fast the winds move.

2. Communicate directly with the ones who can make the change and *ask* for the change you want.

3. By dealing directly with Devas we can influence our weather.

In the same way we can work with the water Devas. When there are storms at sea they are caused by high winds that stir up the waves. By working with the air Devas and water Devas together storms can be lessened. This does not mean we should stop all storms because some wave activity is needed to keep the water stirred up, at least to a certain degree because that is how air, particularly oxygen, gets into the water. The water and air Devas working together ensure that enough oxygen is in the water to support all life in the water that does not come to the surface to breathe air.

Please understand, I was only the spokesperson in the field of collective consciousness voicing the desire of the millions that were in fear and praying. By talking directly to the air Devas, they got the message, shifting their focus from the thrill they were experiencing, to the harm they were about to do. I can't help but wonder if this process just described had been used sooner, if the damage in the Caribbean, Porte Rico and Cuba areas could have been minimized.

Extreme weather and climate change is part of what we are currently going through in Earth's ascension. In the meditative state we can talk to the air Devas, or the water Devas in case of potential flooding, and make our weather less extreme. This can make Earth changes less harsh for people, and nature, everywhere and not just in our area.

We can ask the air Devas to create high-pressure zones that can block cold fronts, or extremely hot weather from coming into our area. If an area is in a drought, ask the Devas to please send rain. If the ground is saturated because you had too much rain, ask them to divert future rain and to send you cloudless skies to help dry up standing water.

It is suggested that before you reach out to the Devas, go into mediation and connect with the field of energy coming from the consciousness of the people and nature (vegetation, animals, soils) that are going to be affected from what you are going to be asking for, so you can be sure this is what they want. This way you can be certain you are their spokesperson. Group energy is much more powerful than trying to do it alone. It is time for us to begin walking in two worlds, the physical world and the spirit world, drawing the two together and creating something greater than either one can separately.

Air and water Devas are not stationary. They move with a massive air or the flow of water. With the ocean currents that so greatly influence our weather, each current has many crews of Devas working with it. Additionally, in those waters there would be many other types of Devas working with the aquatic life that existed in these currents.

Each form of matter, both animate and inanimate, have Devas that work exclusively with that frequency of matter. Earth has between one million and two million different life forms, plus many inanimate forms, each with its own unique Devas. This means that there are millions of types of Devas and countless trillions that make up the Devic kingdom here on Earth! I am hoping you are sensing how important and helpful it could be to you, to us as a human race and the planet, to sense the Devas' presence and begin communicating and working with them.

A fun way to do this is, if you are sitting on a beach relaxing on a sunny day and looking out over the water. If you squint your eyes you may see what look like little sparkles of light dancing above the water. These are air Devas and you may talk to them with your mind and if you are open to receive they may respond.

If you are snorkeling and looking down into the water, or if you are a scuba diving and are in a relaxed and open state of mind you may also see specs of light. These are the water Devas and you can communicate with them, too. A suggestion would be to express your gratitude for the air that you are breathing and for bringing the warmth of the sun you are feeling on your skin.

If you are swimming, bless the water and express gratitude for the pleasure it is bringing you. As you drink a glass of water bless it and fill it with light and love. This water is going to become a part of your blood and tissue in your body, so the end effect is the light and love are going to become a part of you. You may do the same with the food before you eat it. When you do this, you can actually feel the frequency of your physical, mental, and emotional bodies change.

Know, too, that a similar change is taking place in the Devas who are the ones hearing and responding to your thoughts and feelings. In essence you are extending a welcome to them, as they are about to become a part of your physical body. Because your soul has more of the creator's energy and it is a higher frequency, the Deva in your food or drink may be in awe of you.

So be sure to thank them and in turn be open to them because in your body they are going to experience the highest frequencies they have perhaps ever experienced. This is going to help them raise their frequency and they may even become a different, more evolved Deva because of what they experience in your physical body.

When you take anything into your physical body, air, water, or solid food, you are also ingesting the Deva that is their soul essence. The Deva feels and senses the presence of your soul, which is the highest frequency of any physical life form on the planet. The Deva can communicate with your divine soul and if it desires may ask to stay and become a member of a diva family that is working with one of your body's organs or other components.

Your divine soul will decide if the diva is ready for this new role and if and where your body might best benefit from its service. Your divine soul, which is an aspect of the universal creator, is reaching out and touching the Deva, which is the soul aspect of the water, air or solid food which is a lower aspect of the creator.

When you quiet your mind and relax your body and focus your attention within, you may communicate with the many Devas that live within your physical body. Each major organ in your body, brain, heart, lungs, liver, etc., has highly evolved Devas that are the spiritual foundation upon which that physical organ is built. The Devas responsibility is to keep the organ healthy and functioning as it was designed to function.

All lesser organs in your body also have Devas. In the meditative state you may communicate with these Devas telling them what you would like them to do or stop doing. In this way you can take a conscious control of many of the functions of your body. This can be especially helpful if you are undergoing a physical challenge. You can play an active role in healing yourself with the help of your Devas.

In communicating with the Devas in your physical body you are connecting your divine essence to the divine essence, which is the Deva or Devas. In the Bible it states that God created man in his own image and likeness, in his image and likeness he created them. This does not mean that we look like God, rather that we were designed to carry the highest divine frequencies within our physical vehicle, giving us greater potential to be more God-like.

One way to look at our soul, which is the divine essence of the creator, out of which our physical body is made, is our soul can be viewed as "the king of Devas" in our bodies. Devas within us carrying a lesser amount of divine essence would look upon our soul in the same way we might look upon God. That is with reverence and respect and a desire to please. As we grow in our awareness of the Devas in our life, including our food, our drinking water and the air we breathe, reaching out to them and working as one with them, we become in charge of our immediate environment. We then truly are functioning as the creators we are meant to be.

Sometimes you may catch real quick glimpses of nature Devas out of the corner of your eye, but when you look there is nothing there. You know that something was there, and you just missed seeing it. This happens most often to people who have a greater than average sensitivity and often have Crystal energy. These are the same type of people that on occasion see Devas.

People that are emotionally sensitive may feel the energy that the Devas emit and will often smile, because they sense their joy and love. Devas appear to be very peaceful in complete harmony with the world of nature, which is the world in which they live. People that can see Devas often see them on or near plants, especially ones that are blooming. Devas seem to love the beauty and aroma of blooming plants and when they sense the presence of a plant lover they are more apt to make themselves visible to that person.

Earlier in this book I stated that all physical creation is made out of electromagnetic energy and built on a foundation of spiritual energy and consciousness. There is a spiritual foundation under everything physical. The Devas are the divine aspect of everything in nature. This means that Devas are a part of everything that is mineral, liquid, and gas.

Pan, the archangel who is responsible for the entire Devic realm on Earth, its organization, structure and function, heads the Deva kingdom. There are various levels of supervisors and workers and they specialized in things like plants, animals, human physical bodies, gases, and minerals.

All levels of Devas have consciousness and have the ability to be aware of our thoughts, desires, and feelings. This means we are communicating with them during all our waking time, usually without being consciously aware of it. Whatever thoughts and emotions we are holding, they will try to bring it into our physical reality. This is why it is so important to hold in our mind and heart only those things, events, situations, circumstances that we desire and not those things that we fear or do not want.

If you are holding a thought in your mind and empowering it with an emotion, both positive and negative, Devas assume that is what you want. Because they see us in a manner similar to how we see God, they have a great desire to please us and thus help to bring to us what we are holding in our minds and hearts. If you consciously want to communicate with them it can best be done in the meditative state using the language of the subconscious, which is visualization coupled with positive emotion.

My wife and I enjoy their energy, especially when we look out our large bay window in the kitchen that overlooks a beautiful flower garden. In the summer there are usually about 30 plants blooming at any given time. Sitting at the kitchen table looking over the garden we can feel the energy of Devas and when in the garden the energy is even stronger. This energy of joy, love, peace is rejuvenating.

Neighbors out for a walk often stop and spend time in our garden. I don't think they fully understand what the appeal is. They simply see the beauty and that attracts them, but when they leave you can sense their energy and auras are brighter and happier. We host a spiritual metaphysical class at our home every month called The Mystery School.

When the students walk by the garden they always pause, look and smile. You can see and sense their demeanor; energetic frequency and aura are uplifted. Devic energy is most easily felt in nature, especially around large bodies of water, gardens and forests. This is where people are most apt to see and feel Devas. Devic energy is everywhere, in, on and above Earth. When you find an area where you feel it most, go there often, linger there, enjoy yourself, talk to the Devas, and thank them. For some it will be the woods, or mountains, or seashore. For others it may be walking in the wind, sailing or scuba diving.

Plants produce oxygen and absorb carbon dioxide. Both functions are essential for animal and human life. Devas put moisture into the atmosphere that helps to form clouds that produce rain that nourish the plant and animal kingdoms. The plants provide food for both us and for the animal kingdom. The animal kingdoms provide food for us and for carnivorous animals. We in turn plant, cultivate, and fertilize plants. There are many such cycles like this that make our world function. Devas are working hand in hand to provide an environment in which a vast variety of life can flourish.

Animals also have Devas. Devas are the soul foundation for the entire animal kingdom. Each animal will have a whole cadre of Devas just as we do. Their function is to direct the life force energy to the cells and organs in their physical bodies. When that animal dies the Devas do not die but are reassigned usually to a new animal that has just been conceived. As Devas evolve and grow they will be assigned to ever more complex life forms. Like everything in creation Devas also are evolving.

Without the Devas life is not possible on Earth. Because Devas are not sensed by any of our five senses their presence and work are largely unknown by most people. However, all indigenous cultures who live in harmony with nature were aware of Devas, though their names for them varied.

I also hope that you have been motivated to begin communicating with them, asking them for help with your physical body, your garden, the weather and even minimizing the power of things like tornadoes, earthquakes, and hurricanes. Please send them love and gratitude, expressing your appreciation for all that they do for you and your loved ones.

By working hand in hand with them we are greatly empowered, and they greatly appreciate the opportunity to be of service to us. And when communicating with them please do not tell them what you don't want. They will not hear the 'don't' word and are apt to give you the thing you don't want. Please ask only for the outcome you desire.

If you are a light worker, it could be most helpful if you ask for and work toward being able to sense the presence of the Devas and begin working with them in the meditative state. They can enrich anyone's life, allowing you to accomplish so much more with your time and energy. It is hard to sense their presence and not smile because they radiate so much joy.

Many of the Crystal children are able to see, hear, and feel their beautiful energy and when they do you can see them smile or hear them laugh. They make wonderful playmates for these delightful sensitive children. Communicating and working with the Devas not only benefits you but allows you to be helpful to many others.

You can bring or send healing energy to their physical, mental or emotional body. In doing this you are bringing much gratification to the Devas by recognizing their presence and asking for their help. Because they look up to you almost as a

God, they feel honored to be in your presence and recognized by you, so you are creating a win-win situation.

Some people consider Devas to be a part of the angelic realm because they are made out of energy similar to the angels. Angels vibrate at a higher frequency than the Devas but there can be an overlap in the frequencies. They both work with joy, love, compassion and have a strong desire to be helpful to others. This is a different type of energy and at a higher frequency than the electromagnetic energy our physical bodies and planet are made from.

Our emotional body, even though it is housed in a physical body, is aware of and works with some of these same energies. It is through our emotional body, aided by the subconscious part of our mental body, that we can become aware of the angels and Devas that are working with us even though our physical eyes cannot see them.

Because Devas and angels are made of similar energy, when a Deva has learned all that it can learn to be a Deva, it can ask to be considered for training to become an angel. If deemed ready they will be chosen to go into one of the archangel's learning centers and will graduate as an angel.